"Iain Duguid takes a book of the Bible that many Christians are intimidated by and showcases it in its rightful place as the finest of songs. Perhaps we've been as insecure about tackling the allegorical and literal interpretations in this song as we may be in our own relationships. Not anymore! This commentary will prove that of all the songs written to explore the age-old questions of love, the Song of Songs is the one that we cannot and do not want to get out of our heads."

—**Aimee Byrd**, Author, *Housewife Theologian* and *Theological Fitness;* cohost, Mortification of Spin

"So is the Song of Songs really about sex or Jesus? Iain Duguid steers a wise and pastoral path between those simplistic choices. He demonstrates how this poetic book on the excellencies of human love is not merely a practical marriage guide nor an allegorical representation of the coming Christ. Rather, this book is the best song of all songs because it provides divinely inspired insights into the blessings and weaknesses of human love in order to point us toward the goodness and necessity of the grace of God, whose love is perfected in Christ alone."

—**Bryan Chapell**, Pastor, Grace Presbyterian Church, Peoria, Illinois

"Here's the work of a multigifted scholar on display! Here Iain Duguid is the expositor, the biblical theologian, the pastor, the counselor, and—quite often!—the surgeon. This exposition is vintage Duguid—sneakingly convicting and awash in grace. He lures me to oversimplify: if someone asks me how best to prepare for marriage, I will be tempted to say, 'Study the Song of Songs and read Duguid's commentary.'"

—**Dale Ralph Davis**, Minister in Residence, The First Presbyterian Church of Columbia, Columbia, South Carolina

"This book helps us. As a wise and seasoned pastor, Iain gently weeps with us in our broken search for false loves. Yet he strongly rouses our affections to the One whose love is true, satisfying, lasting, romantic, and alluring. Practical, tasty, and invigorating, Iain's prose and poetry offer a timely guide for those who desire the lovers of Solomon's Song to disciple them in Jesus."

—**Zack Eswine**, Pastor, Riverside Church, Webster Groves, Missouri; Director of Homiletics, Covenant Theological Seminary

"Iain Duguid's *Song of Songs* is not your typical commentary. Though based on solid scholarship, it is completely pastoral in tone, easy to read, and rich with insights. Dr. Duguid's pastoral experience anticipates the modern reader's experiences and concerns, and helps us avoid reading the Song of Songs strictly as an allegory or, alternately, as a dating or sex manual. Instead, *Song of Songs* teaches us to appreciate the beauty of married sexual love, while at the very same time enriching our understanding of God's love for us."

—**Winston T. Smith**, Faculty and Counselor, Christian Counseling & Educational Foundation, Glenside, Pennsylvania

Song of Songs

REFORMED EXPOSITORY COMMENTARY

A Series

Song of Songs

Iain M. Duguid

P&R
P U B L I S H I N G
P.O. BOX 817 • PHILLIPSBURG • NEW JERSEY 08865-0817

Italics within Scripture quotations indicate emphasis added.

ISBN: 978-1-59638-948-9 (cloth)
ISBN: 978-1-59638-949-6 (ePub)
ISBN: 978-1-59638-950-2 (Mobi)

Printed in the United States of America

Library of Congress Cataloging-in-Publication Data

Duguid, Iain M.
Song of Songs / Iain M. Duguid.
pages cm. -- (Reformed expository commentary)
Includes bibliographical references and index.
ISBN 978-1-59638-948-9 (hardcover) -- ISBN 978-1-59638-949-6 (epub) -- ISBN 978-1-59638-950-2 (mobi)
1. Bible. Song of Solomon--Commentaries. I. Title.
BS1485.53.D8399 2016
223'.9077--dc23

2015031769

For Sam and Pat Befus:
An apple tree and a lily of the valley,
Still blooming after all these years.

Contents

Series Introduction

In every generation there is a fresh need for the faithful exposition of God's Word in the church. At the same time, the church must constantly do the work of theology: reflecting on the teaching of Scripture, confessing its doctrines of the Christian faith, and applying them to contemporary culture. We believe that these two tasks—the expositional and the theological—are interdependent. Our doctrine must derive from the biblical text, and our understanding of any particular passage of Scripture must arise from the doctrine taught in Scripture as a whole.

We further believe that these interdependent tasks of biblical exposition and theological reflection are best undertaken in the church, and most specifically in the pulpits of the church. This is all the more true since the study of Scripture properly results in doxology and praxis—that is, in praise to God and practical application in the lives of believers. In pursuit of these ends, we are pleased to present the Reformed Expository Commentary as a fresh exposition of Scripture for our generation in the church. We hope and pray that pastors, teachers, Bible study leaders, and many others will find this series to be a faithful, inspiring, and useful resource for the study of God's infallible, inerrant Word.

The Reformed Expository Commentary has four fundamental commitments. First, these commentaries aim to be *biblical*, presenting a comprehensive exposition characterized by careful attention to the details of the text. They are not exegetical commentaries—commenting word by word or even verse by verse—but integrated expositions of whole passages of Scripture. Each commentary will thus present a sequential, systematic treatment of an entire book of the Bible, passage by passage. Second, these commentaries are unashamedly *doctrinal*. We are committed to the Westminster Confession of Faith and Catechisms as containing the system of doctrine taught in the Scriptures of the Old and New Testaments. Each volume will teach, promote, and defend the doctrines of the Reformed faith as they are found in the Bible. Third, these commentaries are *redemptive-historical* in their orientation. We believe in the unity of the Bible and its central message of salvation in Christ. We are thus committed to a Christ-centered view of the Old Testament, in which its characters, events, regulations, and institutions are properly understood as pointing us to Christ and his gospel, as well as giving us examples to follow in living by faith. Fourth, these commentaries are *practical*, applying the text of Scripture to contemporary challenges of life—both public and private—with appropriate illustrations.

The contributors to the Reformed Expository Commentary are all pastor-scholars. As pastor, each author will first present his expositions in the pulpit ministry of his church. This means that these commentaries are rooted in the teaching of Scripture to real people in the church. While aiming to be scholarly, these expositions are not academic. Our intent is to be faithful, clear, and helpful to Christians who possess various levels of biblical and theological training—as should be true in any effective pulpit ministry. Inevitably this means that some issues of academic interest will not be covered. Nevertheless, we aim to achieve a responsible level of scholarship, seeking to promote and model this for pastors and other teachers in the church. Significant exegetical and theological difficulties, along with such historical and cultural background as is relevant to the text, will be treated with care.

We strive for a high standard of enduring excellence. This begins with the selection of the authors, all of whom have proved to be outstanding communicators of God's Word. But this pursuit of excellence is also reflected in a disciplined editorial process. Each volume is edited by both a series editor and a testament editor. The testament editors, Iain Duguid for the Old Testament and Daniel Doriani for the New Testament, are accomplished pastors and respected scholars who have taught at the seminary level. Their job is to ensure that each volume is sufficiently conversant with up-to-date scholarship and is faithful and accurate in its exposition of the text. As series editors, we oversee each volume to ensure its overall quality—including excellence of writing, soundness of teaching, and usefulness in application. Working together as an editorial team, along with the publisher, we are devoted to ensuring that these are the best commentaries that our gifted authors can provide, so that the church will be served with trustworthy and exemplary expositions of God's Word.

It is our goal and prayer that the Reformed Expository Commentary will serve the church by renewing confidence in the clarity and power of Scripture and by upholding the great doctrinal heritage of the Reformed faith. We hope that pastors who read these commentaries will be encouraged in their own expository preaching ministry, which we believe to be the best and most biblical pattern for teaching God's Word in the church. We hope that lay teachers will find these commentaries among the most useful resources they rely on for understanding and presenting the text of the Bible. And we hope that the devotional quality of these studies of Scripture will instruct and inspire each Christian who reads them in joyful, obedient discipleship to Jesus Christ.

May the Lord bless all who read the Reformed Expository Commentary. We commit these volumes to the Lord Jesus Christ, praying that the Holy Spirit will use them for the instruction and edification of the church, with thanksgiving to God the Father for his unceasing faithfulness in building his church through the ministry of his Word.

Richard D. Phillips
Philip Graham Ryken
Series Editors

Preface

There would be no sermons without congregations. That may not be completely true: I did meet a church planter who once delivered a sermon to an entirely empty auditorium because no one turned up for the service (his own family happened to be out of town that week). He preached the message aloud anyway because he felt that even if no one else needed to hear his sermon on faith, he himself certainly did! But the exception underlines the rule. Preachers need listeners, and good listeners are a tremendous encouragement to those of us who preach. I would therefore like to thank the congregation of Christ Presbyterian Church, Grove City, Pennsylvania, for providing such an attentive audience for these sermons. The fledgling congregation of Christ Presbyterian Church, Philadelphia, was also remarkably eager to have this book as the topic for our first sermon series, which would not exactly be conventional church-planting wisdom.

Many individuals within those congregations encouraged us along the way, and it is risky to single some out and risk slighting others who were equally important. But Matt & Rebecca Harmon and Jonathan & Kat Kuciemba formed a wonderful pastoral team with us in Grove City, along with our elders and deacons. We look forward to continuing our relationship with them as our overseeing session, and with Lincoln & Emma Larsen as he joins the team in Philadelphia as an intern. One other couple from Grove City stand out as a particular inspiration: our friends Bob & Louise Schmidtberger share a love that has endured many trials and difficulties unquenched: their unfailing care for others and constant encouragement of us and of the church are hard to leave behind.

I would also like to thank those who have contributed to the production of this volume: Phil Ryken and Doug O'Donnell read the manuscript carefully and corrected many mistakes, while Amanda Martin and John J. Hughes, along with the whole team at P&R Publishing, skillfully brought it into its finished form.

It has been poignant to ponder this material as we contemplate our own children's reaching the age where love and marriage become the source of so much potential joy and frustration. We pray for Wayne, Jamie, Sam & Peggy, Hannah, Rob, and Rosie & Chris that they will find great joy in the Lord's plans for them in this area of life, whether that involves marriage or singleness. I would also like to thank Barb, for excelling as a wife who constantly cares about our relationship and pursues me, even when I am so far from being the ideal husband. I am richly blessed to be married to a woman who understands grace so deeply.

I would like to dedicate this book to Barb's parents, Sam and Pat Befus. They are a couple whose faithful love has been lifelong and unfaltering, and whose lives were poured out in service of the church, first as missionaries in Asia, Africa, and South America, and then in pastoral ministry closer to home. They are real people with real faults and failings, but also a very deep and genuine love for the Lord and for those around them. Everyone who has known them has been profoundly touched by the warmth of their love; I owe them a personal debt of gratitude for welcoming me into their family so kindly more than thirty years ago, and for praying for us and cheering us on ever since.

Introduction[1]

What on earth is the Song of Songs about? If that is your response to this biblical book, then you are certainly not alone. A British Old Testament scholar, David Clines, used to assign the book to his entering class of university students, along with the question, "What does the Book do to you if you read it? (Be intellectual about this, not confessional)." One student said, "Personally, I would like a narrative alongside this text to explain what is actually happening. I find it to be slightly confusing and annoying that what is happening is never clear," while another commented, "I have a nose like the tower of Lebanon and like the Great Wall of China, but I do not consider it worthy of romantic poetry."[2] It is certainly a challenging book to understand.

Interpreting the Song

Part of the difficulty of the Song of Songs comes from the fact that it is a *song*, and therefore poetry. Poetry is the art of condensation: expressing maximum meaning in the minimum number of words. As a result, poetry is often more evocative than explicative. It doesn't take the time to unpack its figures of speech or to explain its analogies. It relies on the reader to fill in the blanks. Poetry tends to be open-ended, leaving us pondering and wondering rather than tying up every loose end with a watertight argument.

1. I have written a much lengthier discussion of these introductory matters in *The Song of Songs: An Introduction and Commentary*, TOTC 19 (Downers Grove, IL: InterVarsity Press, 2015), 19–56. Here I will simply summarize my conclusions from that work.

2. D. J. A. Clines, "Why Is There a Song of Songs and What Does It Do to You If You Read It?," in *Interested Parties: The Ideology of Writers and Readers of the Hebrew Bible*, ed. P. R. Davies and D. J. A. Clines, JSOTS 205 (Sheffield, UK: Sheffield Academic Press, 1995), 94–121.

Yet at the same time, poetry has a remarkable ability to address the whole person and to move our souls with a power that prose can rarely match.

The second challenge is to decide what precisely the Song is about. On one level, that is an easy question to answer: it is about love. But whose love? Some scholars have argued that it is an originally secular love song about two people that acquired a religious cast simply by being included in the Bible. On the opposite end of the spectrum, others have insisted that it was composed as an allegory of God's love for his people that really has nothing to do with human love at all.

Historically speaking, an allegorical approach that sees the Song of Songs as being about the love of God for his people has certainly been the most popular among preachers. It is not hard to see why. Without having to descend to the embarrassing matter of talking about sex from the pulpit, hearers can be encouraged and directed in their spiritual lives with all kinds of edifying observations about prayer and Bible reading. Don't worry: it is all about Jesus! So according to Cyril of Alexandria, writing in the fifth century A.D., when the woman describes her lover lying between her two breasts like a sachet of myrrh, what she is really talking about is Jesus coming between the two Testaments, Old and New. This allegorical approach enabled Bernard of Clairvaux to preach eighty-six sermons on the opening chapters of the Song of Songs to a congregation of monks!

Graeme Goldsworthy illustrates the problem of this approach, however, by the example of the Australian Sunday school teacher who was concerned that her lessons were becoming too predictable. So one week she started out by asking her children, "What's gray, furry and lives in eucalyptus trees?" No response. So she asked again. Still no response. In desperation, she asked the pastor's daughter, "Suzie, don't you know what the answer is?" She replied slowly, "Miss, I know the answer must be Jesus, but it sure sounds like a koala to me."[3] Sometimes a koala really is just a koala, not a picture of Jesus.

The kind of free association that Cyril of Alexandria engaged in is, of course, the problem with allegorical interpretation. Given enough imagination, you can get radically different messages out of the same passage: the Song can relate to Yahweh and Israel, God and the church, or wisdom and the individual soul. Equally, you can get the same message out of radically different passages: in that case, why do we need the Bible at all, when by

3. Graeme Goldsworthy, *Preaching the Whole Bible as Christian Scripture* (Grand Rapids: Eerdmans, 2000), xi.

using the same technique you could preach edifying messages from *Winnie the Pooh*?

On the other hand, a more typological form of interpretation pays attention to inner biblical connections. It sees the hero of the Song as Solomon, the son of David, the king of Israel. If that is the case, then it is not just a random connection to see the man as pointing to Christ and his bride as pointing to the church. Other biblical passages seem self-evidently to point beyond themselves to a coming greater Son of David, even if they were originally written for Solomon or another Old Testament king—for example, Psalm 45, a psalm written for a royal wedding, and Psalm 72, which speaks of the Son of David's ruling from shore to shore.

There are two potential dangers with such a typological approach, however. The first is that in its eagerness to draw positive connections between the hero of the Song and Christ, it might overemphasize the similarities between them and overlook the differences. In practice, this tendency frequently pushes typology in the direction of the free-association kind of allegory in order to find Christ in the passage. The other problem is that this approach tends to downplay or even ignore the specifics of the surface-level meaning of the text in favor of a general connection to Christ. The message that a passage such as Psalm 72 might have had for the Davidic kings themselves, or even for us as we think about our own rulers and political structures, gets completely lost. So, too, any message that the Song of Songs might have about human relationships and earthly marriage tends to get lost or downplayed in favor of its immediate application to the relationship of Christ and the individual believer.

In response to this approach, other preachers have interpreted the Song of Songs simply as a celebration of human love and sex. Instead of comparing it to passages such as Psalm 45, they read the Song against the backdrop of passages such as Proverbs 5, in which the father says to the son, "Rejoice in the wife of your youth, a lovely deer, a graceful doe. Let her breasts fill you at all times with delight; be intoxicated always in her love. Why should you be intoxicated, my son, with a forbidden woman and embrace the bosom of an adulteress?" (Prov. 5:18–20). We might call this the "Solomon on sex" approach to the Song, to quote the title of one popular book.[4] The Song now becomes simply a divine dating and marriage-counseling manual. To use the Goldsworthy analogy, this time the koala is just a koala, and the Sunday

4. Joseph Dillow, *Solomon on Sex* (Nashville: Thomas Nelson, 1982).

school lesson becomes simply a Christian biology class about the birds and the koalas. In the process, the applications to human relationships can become as imaginative and strained as anything ever dreamed up by the earlier allegorists.

There is certainly nothing wrong with biology classes or practical tips about dating and marriage. But when Jesus unpacked the central message of the Old Testament to his disciples on the road to Emmaus, he didn't focus on its value in providing practical teaching for their marriages. He declared that the central message of the Old Testament is the sufferings of Christ and the glories that will follow—that is, the gospel.[5] What is more, the title of the book, "The Song of Songs,"[6] is a superlative: it indicates that this poem is the finest of songs, in the same way that the Holy of Holies was the very holiest of places in the temple. Is human love, even within marriage, the worthy subject of the very best of songs? The Bible tells us that true love is not that we love one another, nor even that we love God. Rather, it is that God loved us and sent his Son as the atoning sacrifice for our sins (1 John 4:10). So the finest of songs surely has to point us in some profound way to God's love for us in Christ, the love that entered our fallen world, lived the perfect life in our place, and suffered and died for our sins.

In fact, even a passage such as Proverbs 5 is not merely about human faithfulness in marriage, because as we read on in Proverbs we discover that the fundamental choice that faces all of us in life lies between Dame Wisdom, whose home is built on the foundation of the fear of the Lord, and Lady Folly, who seduces fools away from true worship to the worship of idols. Adultery is never just about sex in the book of Proverbs, any more than the idea of "building a house" in that book is just about bricks and mortar.

I believe that it is possible to steer a middle ground between the allegorical and literal extremes: to recognize the Song of Songs as wisdom literature that celebrates a great mystery in life, the mutual love of a man and a woman (Prov. 30:19), yet that in this celebration will not only shape our thinking about human relationships but also show us profound insights into the love that Christ has for his bride, the church. To change the Goldsworthy analogy, suppose that the Sunday school teacher had described a sparrow and

5. See Iain M. Duguid, *Is Jesus in the Old Testament?* (Phillipsburg, NJ: P&R Publishing, 2013).

6. This biblical book is sometimes referred to as "The Song of Solomon." Both titles are abbreviations of the fuller title in the superscription of the book itself, which is literally "The Song of Songs, about that which belongs to Solomon." Given the complexity of determining the relationship of Solomon to the Song, which I discuss in more detail below, I have chosen to use the simpler title, "The Song of Songs."

then gone on to teach her students about God's care for the little sparrow and his far greater fatherly care for us. The sparrow is not Jesus; it remains just a sparrow. Yet the lesson that is drawn from the sparrow can and must still center appropriately on Jesus, as the One who shows us the full extent of God's fatherly love and care for us. So, too, we don't need to make the man in the Song of Songs into an allegory or a type of Jesus to see how the book points us to "the sufferings of Christ and the glories that will follow."

SOLOMON IN THE SONG

Then there is the question of the role of Solomon in the Song. Is Solomon the author and hero of the story? Many fine commentators think so, both among those who follow the allegorical or typological model and among those who follow the literal model. The opening superscription might seem to point clearly in that direction.[7] Isn't the greatest Davidic king the ideal person to speak about love and marriage, and thus foreshadow Christ? But that identification seems difficult to reconcile with the historical Solomon that we know from the rest of the Bible—a famous collector of a thousand wives and concubines (1 Kings 11:3). He hardly seems like a model of an exclusive, lifelong, "till death do us part" marriage relationship, the kind extolled in the Song! Even if Solomon wrote the book to a particular woman when he was young, before he married all his other wives, his subsequent life story would surely undercut the Song's teaching. What would we say about someone who gave a wonderful testimony in church about his true love for his bride—and then later repeatedly betrayed her trust? Would we keep that testimony prominently posted on our church website, even if everything he had said about love and marriage were true?

Similar difficulties attend the view that Solomon wrote the Song later in life as an act of repentance. That might work if he wrote it about someone else, but it would hardly be an act of repentance to speak about the wonderful love he had shared with his one and only true love while omitting any mention of his own long subsequent history of serial adultery. People can certainly teach us how to do things that they themselves have not done very

7. The evidence, however, is not as clear as it might superficially seem. In Hebrew, the superscription actually deviates markedly from the normal ascription of authorship seen in the Psalms, suggesting a more complex relationship between Solomon and the Song. For a fuller discussion, see Duguid, *The Song of Songs*, 73–76.

well, but if they pretend that they did them perfectly themselves when they didn't, that is a problem.

There are other issues with seeing the hero of the Song as Solomon. If Solomon is the hero of the Song, how would the Shulammite's love for her man illustrate the theme that is so central to chapter 8, that true love cannot be bought for any price? When someone is about to marry one of the richest men in the world, allow me to be skeptical of the purity of her motives. This is like Elizabeth Bennet in *Pride and Prejudice* suddenly deciding that perhaps Mr. Darcy isn't so sullen and proud, immediately after she sees his gorgeous estate in Derbyshire! Moreover, if Solomon wrote the Song of Songs about himself, then the wonderful description of the man's appearance in 5:10–16 seems an embarrassingly laudatory self-portrait.

Some commentators have therefore imagined that the Song depicts a three-cornered love triangle between Solomon, the woman, and her shepherd-boy lover. In this approach, Solomon has carried the woman off to his harem, but she pines for (and in some cases actually pursues) her true love. Yet this view requires abrupt transitions in the poems from one subject to another, not to mention raising acute moral and ethical questions about a woman who is married to one man (however unwillingly) and actively pursuing a love relationship with someone else.

For these reasons, I take the Song of Songs to be a poem by an unknown and anonymous author about two idealized people, a man and a woman, whose exclusive and committed love is great but, like all loves in this fallen world, far from perfect. As we will see, their idealized love story is actually contrasted in the Song with the alternative Solomonic model of "love," clearly displayed in 1 Kings 11. This Solomonic model identifies love as a commercial and political transaction, serving as a means to some other end, whether wealth, political advantage, security, or significance. Thus, the Song is designed to show each of us how far short of perfection we fall, both as humans and as lovers, and to drive us into the arms of our true heavenly Husband, Jesus Christ, whose love for his bride is truly perfect. Solomon is thus a foil for the main character, not the main character himself.

Finally, a word about the structure of the Song. Some scholars have denied any unity to the Song, seeing it as a very loose anthology of love poems, while at the opposite extreme, others have suggested that it forms a tightly structured chiasm. I think the answer lies somewhere in between. As we noted earlier, the title given in the first verse, the "Song of Songs," is a superlative, "the Finest of Songs." That suggests that this is not an anthology made up of many different songs, but rather that at its heart it is one song. That is not to say that the poem tells a straightforward sequential narrative, but there is general agreement among commentators about the broad outlines of the Song. After the superscription, there are six major units: 1:2–2:7; 2:8–3:5; 3:6–5:1; 5:2–6:3; 6:4–8:4; 8:5–14.[8] The opening and closing sections of the Song balance one another with a number of significant verbal parallels, while the section 3:6–5:1, which includes the consummation of the marriage, forms the central core for the piece.

It does seem, therefore, that there is a broad development of and logical flow to the Song. In general, this movement leads up to and away from the marriage and the consummation of the relationship, a flow that makes it possible to speak of *before* and *after* in the couple's interactions. Unlike Hollywood stories, which typically focus exclusively on the excitement of the *before* phase of the relationship, the Song shows us some aspects of the ongoing relationship *after* the wedding as well, while still leaving the couple (and us) at the end of the Song longing for something more complete—a more perfect and eternally enduring love.

Outline

1. Title (1:1)

2. Prologue (1:2–2:7)
    A. Introduction (1:2–14)
        i. Desire (1:2–4)
        ii. Uncertainty and Request (1:5–7)
        iii. Response and Reassurance (1:8–11)
        iv. Desire (1:12–14)
    B. A Litany of Love (1:15–2:7)
        i. Mutual Affirmation (1:15–2:3)
        ii. The Delights and Dangers of Love (2:4–7)

8. See J. Cheryl Exum, *Song of Songs: A Commentary*, OTL (Louisville: Westminster John Knox, 2005), 38. Many of the divisions between the units are marked by the appearance of particular terms, such as "come"; "house," "room," or garden"; "wine"; and "embrace" (Richard S. Hess, *Song of Songs*, BCOTWP [Grand Rapids: Baker Academic, 2005], 31), while the repeated refrains about not stirring up love form clear structural markers (2:7; 3:5; 8:4).

3. Before the Wedding: Joined and Separated (2:8–3:5)
    A. Morning (2:8–17)
    B. Night (3:1–5)

4. The Wedding (3:6–5:1)
    A. Question (3:6)
    B. Solomon's Glory (3:7–11)
    C. The Beloved's Glory (4:1–7)
    D. Consummation (4:8–5:1)

5. After the Wedding: Separated and Rejoined (5:2–6:3)
    A. Night (5:2–8)
    B. The Lover's Glory (5:9–16)
    C. Restoration (6:1–3)

6. Contemplation and Renewed Consummation (6:4–8:4)
    A. Contemplation of the Beloved (6:4–10)
    B. Response (6:11–12)
    C. Contemplation of the Beloved (6:13–7:10a)
    D. Response (7:10b–11)
    E. Renewed Consummation (7:12–8:4)

7. Epilogue (8:5–14)
    A. The Overwhelming Power of Love (8:5–7)
    B. The Incomparable Value of Love (8:8–12)
    C. The Unending Nature of Love (8:13–14)

Abbreviations

AOTC	Apollos Old Testament Commentary
ATR	*Anglican Theological Review*
BCOTWP	Baker Commentary on the Old Testament Wisdom and Psalms
CT	*Christianity Today*
ESV	English Standard Version
HCSB	Holman Christian Standard Bible
JSOTS	Journal for the Study of the Old Testament Supplements
NASB	New American Standard Bible
NICOT	New International Commentary on the Old Testament
NIV	New International Version
OTL	Old Testament Library
SVT	Supplements to *Vetus Testamentum*
TOTC	Tyndale Old Testament Commentaries

Song of Songs

Friendship on Fire

1

Desire and Satisfaction

Song of Songs 1:1–4

1 The Finest of Songs, about what is Solomon's.[1]

Woman
2 Oh, that he would kiss me with the kisses of his mouth!
For your caresses are better than wine.
3 As for the scent of your oils, it [too] is better.
Your name is flowing oil.
No wonder the eligible young women love you!
4 Carry me off with you, hurry!
Oh, that the king would bring me [to] his chambers!

Daughters of Jerusalem
We will exult and rejoice in you!
We will celebrate your caresses more than wine.

Woman
Rightly they adore you!

It is common for books to have an introduction, in which they set the scene, introduce the main characters, and orient you to the action that will

1. Unless otherwise noted, quotations from the Song of Songs are the author's own translation throughout this volume.

follow. Thus, in Charles Dickens's *Tale of Two Cities*, the author follows his famous first line, "It was the best of times, it was the worst of times," with a lengthy description of the state of society and affairs in England and France that provides the backdrop for the ensuing action. Other authors, however, prefer to launch right into the action. Novelist Iain Banks begins his book *The Crow Road* like this:

> It was the day my Grandmother exploded. I sat in the crematorium, listening to my Uncle Hamish quietly snoring in harmony to Bach's Mass in B Minor, and I reflected that it always seemed to be death that drew me back to Gallanach.[2]

Kiss Me!

The Song of Songs belongs very much to the latter category of composition. It plunges right into its subject matter without introducing the characters, setting the stage, or anything else, with the breathless declaration of the woman: "Oh, that he would kiss me with the kisses of his mouth!" (Song 1:2). Like love itself, the Song of Songs catches us in the midst of life and steals our breath away. The very first words are words of want, of aching desire—for this is what the Song is really about.[3] The Song of Songs is not primarily a book about sex, or a manual of dating tips, or an "agony aunt" column of relationship advice. It is a book about desire from beginning to end—desire stirred, desire frustrated, desire satisfied, desire frustrated again—but above all, desire. The woman wants something—or rather someone—with a passionate and breathless desire.

What she wants from the man is spelled out rather clearly: she longs for the kisses of his mouth. What other kinds of kisses are there, you may ask? Well, apparently Egyptians indulged in rather more formal "nose kisses," which would perhaps be comparable to the "kiss on the cheek" greeting that happens in some cultures.[4] Needless to say, that is not what the woman has in mind.

2. Iain M. Banks, *The Crow Road* (London: Scribners, 1992), 3.

3. See Carey Ellen Walsh, *Exquisite Desire: Religion, the Erotic, and the Song of Songs* (Minneapolis: Fortress, 2000), 8.

4. Michael V. Fox, *The Song of Songs and the Ancient Egyptian Love Songs* (Madison, WI: University of Wisconsin Press, 1985), 97.

Indeed, her thoughts become clearer still when she declares, "Your caresses are better than wine" (Song 1:2). English translations often translate "caresses" rather coyly as "love," but there is no question about what kind of love she has in mind. When this Hebrew word (*dôd*) occurs in the plural, as it does here, sexual intimacy is in view. In Ezekiel 16:8, a young woman who has reached sexual maturity is ready for "love" (*dôdîm*). Likewise, in Proverbs 7:18, the adulteress seduces the young man with the words: "Come, let us take our fill of love [*dôdîm*] till morning." It is thus a particular kind of "love" that she desires from the man: sexual love. Yet at the same time, the word also connotes a particular kind of sex: passionate sex, not simply an act of procreation. She wants the man for himself (and for herself), not just so that she can bear his children. That kind of love, she says, would be better than wine—a symbol of a rich and fulfilling life.

From the taste of his kisses, she moves on to the aroma of his anointing oils (Song 1:3). Scents have a remarkable power to stimulate memories. Whether it is the smell of overcooked cabbage, which brings back years of abominable school meals, or the fragrance of rosewater that reminds you of your grandmother, a single whiff can bring flooding back a raft of associations, good or bad. In this case, when she recalls the aroma of his distinctive cologne, the associations are all good. Even though the man isn't present with her right now—for there is no dialogue in this section—the mere memory of his scent can bring him to be with her in a way that comforts her aloneness.

The Sound of His Name

Yet the woman's attraction to the man is not merely physical. What draws her to him as much as the man's touch or his scent is his name, which she compares to oil that has been poured out (Song 1:3), releasing its fragrance. It isn't simply that her knees grow weak whenever someone says "Fred," or "Jonathan," or "Maher-shalal-hashbaz," or whatever his name happened to be. What makes her feel excited is what that name represents, which is his character. The man is not just a sweet-smelling, good-looking hunk who also happens to be a good kisser; he is reliable and responsible, respected and admired by others in the community as a man of integrity and character.

This is the man whom she loves—and whom she is convinced that everyone else ought to love as well. This is, of course, characteristic of love. It demands to be shared. When your sister or daughter falls hard for the adorable fellow student that she met at college, expect to spend the next several weeks hearing about him. A lot. His cute little habits, the curl in his hair, the summer he spent volunteering in an African orphanage, the picture he has on his cell phone of his beautiful younger sister . . . oh, and did I mention his hair? Nor will she be content until you acknowledge that he is indeed rather a dish. So, too, in the Song, the woman is convinced that her view of the man is shared by all the *ʿalāmôt* (Song 1:3). These are not strictly "virgins," as the ESV translates it, but rather young women who have recently reached the age of sexual maturity and are thus ready for marriage,[5] the people who in every culture tend to be the arbiters of what constitutes male desirability.

Such powerful desire seeks satisfaction. The woman longs for her beloved to sweep her off her feet, and to carry her off swiftly to the privacy and intimacy of his chambers (Song 1:4), where she can finally experience the kisses and caresses for which she so longs. She wants to be able to say those classic lines from the novel *Jane Eyre*, "Reader, I married him." Deep sighs of satisfaction all around as the credits roll. Indeed, in this poem, as the camera fades away from this image of the happy couple, we hear the endorsement of the community on their affection. A plural voice, perhaps representing the daughters of Jerusalem, adds its benediction to their love story, affirming that the approbation of the eligible young women is correct: his caresses are indeed better than wine, and their relationship is truly something to be celebrated. Notice what has not yet transpired, however. The man is not actually present in this scene, except as the object of the woman's desire. He does not actually kiss her, nor do they yet make love. It is not yet clear at this stage whether her longing for a relationship with him is even reciprocated, let alone whether it will ever be consummated.

Reshaping Our Views of Gender

So what does this short poem have to teach us about our own relationships? Immediately, it is clear that the Song intends to challenge and reshape our views of sex, gender, and marriage, whether we have formed those views from the culture around us or from the Christian subculture in which we grew up. Wisdom literature always provides "beams" and "bombs"—the

5. See Richard S. Hess, *Song of Songs*, BCOTWP (Grand Rapids: Baker Academic, 2005), 51–52.

sturdy beams that are the building materials of a Christian worldview and the powerful bombs that explode the false worldviews that we so easily substitute for it.

How does this poem do that? To begin with, the woman is neither a feminist nor a traditionalist. In contrast to our wider culture, which depicts women as equally sexually aggressive as men, she does not dream of grabbing her man, planting a kiss on his lips, and dragging him behind her into her bedroom. She wants *him* to kiss her, and *him* to sweep her off her feet. Yet neither is she a shrinking violet who will pine away in silence, waiting for the man to figure out her interest in him. She expects and longs for the man to provide the leadership in their relationship, while at the same time she is not shy about communicating her own hopes and desires. This contrasts dramatically with much that passes for wisdom within our Christian subculture, which depicts the woman's role in seeking a romantic relationship in purely passive terms.

Likewise, the woman in the Song is neither independent of her community nor completely subject to her family's wishes. She is a strong woman who knows her own mind and what she is seeking in a man. Unlike some young people whom I have counseled, she doesn't need her father's permission before she is able to have a cup of coffee with a young man "alone" (along with six hundred other people!) in a college cafeteria. Yet at the same time, contrary to the trend in our culture, it matters in the Song what the community thinks of their relationship. Love is not its own sufficient reason, regardless of what others think. The woman wants her relationship to be publicly accepted and celebrated by those around her.

Reshaping Our Views of Sex (and How to Present Them)

Equally, the vision of sexuality that is presented in the Song is a long way both from the picture in our culture and from the image that has often been presented in the church. In our culture, any kind of sexual love between any two consenting adults is regarded as good and proper, something to be celebrated whatever their gender or relationship. You don't have to be married or even to be in a long-term committed relationship to engage in intercourse: sex is just sex. Nor is sex just for men and women in our culture: it can be for men and men or for women and women. That is not the perspective that the Song celebrates, as we will see. It glorifies as the ideal human relationship a single-hearted, lifelong, devoted, and exclusive relationship between one man and one woman.

Typically, when Christians talk about why premarital sex, adultery, easy divorce, or homosexuality is wrong, we go straight to the legal passages of the Bible and point to the *thou shalt not*s. Of course, those laws are true and biblical, the loving commands of our heavenly Father, who knows the destructive power of sexual sin in our lives. Yet the Song of Songs reminds us that sometimes it might be better for us to spend more time referencing the *thou shalt*s as well. In the garden of Eden, when Satan asked Eve, "Did God actually say, 'You shall not eat of any tree in the garden'?" (Gen. 3:1), she recounted to him the law about not eating from the forbidden tree, even adding some extra regulations about not touching the tree, just to be on the safe side. But in her focus on the commandment about not eating from one special tree, she downplayed what God had said first: "You may surely eat of every tree of the garden" (2:16). She mentioned the permission, to be sure (3:2), but she missed the emphatic nature of God's command to eat ("You may *surely* eat . . ."), as well as its comprehensive breadth (". . . of *every* tree of the garden"). Those key omissions set her up to believe Satan's lie that God was a restrictive and hard taskmaster rather than a kind and generous Father, and therefore that his law is repressive rather than liberating.

The church has often done the same thing with sex. We have focused on all the ways in which the Bible tells us *not* to have sex, even adding some extra regulations of our own. The early and medieval church glorified virginity and celibacy as higher spiritual states than marriage. Yet when the woman in the Song dreams of her boyfriend, she does not imagine them sharing an inductive Bible study and praying together, but thinks about his kisses and caresses. It is precisely this desire that her community celebrates and rejoices in. Such thoughts are not aberrant and dirty, but good and right. Sex is not merely permissible under the proper circumstances; it is a wonderful and glorious gift in the context for which God designed it, which is within marriage. It is therefore good and right for us to long for it. After all, God himself crafted all the relevant body parts and the various biochemical reactions that make sex such fun. We should celebrate and rejoice in that fact! Even when our desires for sex are unable to be satisfied or are disordered in their object, the desire itself is something that God made good.

This also speaks to the way in which we address those who are struggling with the temptation to engage in premarital sex or with same-sex attraction. It is not enough for us to say that the Bible says that premarital and homosexual sex is wrong, although it does. The law cannot change our hearts. In fact, by itself, the law can only condemn us, often leaving us feeling guilty and dirty, and sometimes driving us away from God rather than toward him. In contrast, the Song paints a glorious picture of the marriage relationship between a man and a woman that is so rich and deep that we should all long to have a relationship just like that. To be sure, as a result of the fall, we all have disordered desires. For some, given their particular makeup and background, that disordered desire will be same-sex attraction. For others, it may be a desire to possess and use members of the opposite gender to serve their own lust, whether that desire is ever acted on or remains concealed in their minds. For still others, the disorder may be a complete suppression of any sexual desire as something dirty and wicked. We are all broken people, and the answer that the Song gives to our sexual brokenness is to show us with incredible beauty what sexual wholeness would actually look like: one man and one woman deeply and permanently bonded together in a unique relationship of love.

The Perfect Bridegroom

What use is a beautiful picture of wholeness when we are all so broken, though? Isn't that like rubbing salt into our wounds, or like seeing a mirage of cool, refreshing water in a dry and thirsty desert? It might be, if the Song of Songs were all that we had in the Bible. Yet the Song echoes the melody of another deeper and richer song, a song about a true and faithful Lover who is not like Solomon, with his massive harem of disposable women, but rather One who loves and gives himself for his bride. Though we are dark and unlovely (see Song 1:6), he is "altogether lovely" (5:16 NIV). This Lover is preparing the church to be his bride, adorning us with the beautiful garments of his spotless righteousness in place of our own filthy rags of sin and failure—including all our sexual failure. He is preparing a honeymoon mansion for us in heaven, where he will spend eternity delighting in us as his chosen beloved. The conclusion of the biblical story is the God of all creation declaring joyously about his church, "Reader, I married her!" He is the true Hero for whom all our hearts yearn, the One toward whom all our most intense earthly desires ultimately point.

This is how the Song speaks to us today, whether we are looking for love, in love, out of love, forsaken and disillusioned by love, or totally confused about the whole subject. Our desire to love and be loved by a human being is at its core simply a reflection of our desperate need to love and be loved by the God who made us for himself. As Augustine famously put it: "You have made our hearts for yourself, O Lord, and our hearts are restless until they find repose in you."[6] The Song addresses us as broken people who have disordered desires and shows us a glimpse of what ordered desire looks like, while at the same time reminding us just how hard it is to find love like that in this world. In so doing, the Song of Songs calls us to a relationship with the One who entered this world of disordered desires and loved perfectly in our place. Jesus Christ is truly the One whose name is above all names. The aroma of Christ and his righteousness fills the world with true sweetness and beauty (2 Cor. 2:14); as Christians, we are all longing for the day when he will come and sweep us off our feet and carry us off to our heavenly home so that our relationship can finally be fulfilled. The intensity of our earthly desire for love thus mirrors that greater and deeper hunger for God's love.

Yet it also works the other way around. The intensity of the heavenly love with which Christ has loved us relativizes all our earthly desires. Jesus loved perfectly as a human being without ever being married, or enjoying the kind of intimacy and sexual pleasure that our hearts and bodies so easily feel that we cannot live well without. This means that if God's perfect plan for us doesn't involve sex and marriage (which always go together in God's plan), we are not somehow less than human or doomed to live unfulfilled and unsatisfied lives. Equally, if we have failed in our sexual or marital history, what counts far more than our record of unfaithfulness is the faithfulness that our heavenly Husband has shown to us. Human marriage is a pointer to Christ's love; if we have the reality, then everything else may fade away.

Responding to God's Love

Do you have that reality in your life? Are you married to Christ through faith in his faithfulness to you, expressed in his obedient life, perfect death,

6. Augustine, *Confessions*, trans. E. B. Pusey (New York: E. P. Dutton & Co., 1949), 1.1 (language updated).

and triumphant resurrection? When God asks why he should let you into his heaven, is your answer "Because I belong, body and soul, to my faithful Husband, Jesus Christ, and I am trusting in his goodness, not my own"?[7] That is the only answer that opens the door to a joy-filled eternity. That answer paves the way to a life of deep joy here on earth as well, in spite of our ongoing brokenness.

If you are married to Christ, is that relationship the center of your thinking? Do you find yourself dreaming about him, lost in amazement at how wonderful Christ is, how incredible it is that he should love you, and longing for more of his presence? Do you constantly wear out your friends and relations with your endless chatter about how wonderful your Beloved is? If you are anything like me, the answer most of the time is "No." I have to admit to living most of the time as a functional single, spiritually speaking. Every now and then I bump into Christ, as it were, and am reminded that we are married. It helps, of course, that as a pastor and professor, reading the Bible is actually my job! Even so, much of the time I am so absorbed with my own earthly desires and projects that I admit to my shame that he never even crosses my mind.

The answer to my sinful self-centeredness is not more law: it is not telling me that I need to spend more time in Bible study, or that I need to pursue longer quiet times, or to endure more rigorous Christian disciplines. The answer to my self-centeredness is worship: beholding the beauty of God in the face of the Lord Jesus Christ. This is why in our church we return to the Lord's Table every week. As we come to the Table, we come afresh to gaze on the beauty of Christ crucified and raised, and to be reminded that even when our gaze wanders away after our other lovers, his gaze remains steadfastly and lovingly fixed on us. At the feast, we remember the glory of Jesus' sacrifice, the excellence of his love for us, and the splendor of the inheritance that is stored up for us in him. Week after week, we join our brothers and sisters and say once again, "We will rejoice and be glad in you! We will celebrate again your love! We will turn our hearts and our faces toward you, O Christ, and proclaim the beauty of your name, which is better than oil that is poured out, sweeter than the richest of wine." There our hearts are fed and our souls refreshed with the good news of his relentless love for us, his beloved bride, as we await his long-expected return.

7. See the Heidelberg Catechism Q. 1. In this paraphrase, I have substituted the word *Husband* for the original *Savior.*

2

Affirmation and Intimacy

Song of Songs 1:5—14

Woman
5 I am dark but beautiful, O daughters of Jerusalem,
like the tents of Kedar, like the curtains of Solomon.
6 Do not stare at me because I am weather-beaten,
because the sun has glared down on me.
The sons of my mother were harsh with me;
they set me as a keeper of the vineyards;
[but] my vineyard—the one which belongs to me—I have not kept.

7 Tell me, you whom my soul loves, where are you shepherding?
Where do you make [your sheep] lie down at noon?
Why should I be like a veiled woman
around the flocks of your companions?

Man
8 If you do not know, O most beautiful of women,
follow the tracks of the sheep
and pasture your young goats
around the dwellings of the shepherds.
9 I compare you to a mare among the chariots of Pharaoh, my darling.
10 Your cheeks are beautiful with earrings,
your neck with strings [of jewels].
11 We will make earrings of gold for you,
with studs of silver.

Woman
12 While the king is on his couch,
my nard gives its scent.
13 My beloved is to me a pouch of myrrh;
between my breasts he will spend the night.
14 My beloved is to me a cluster of henna
in the vineyards of Engedi.

There are basically two contrasting kinds of love stories in the literary world. On the one hand, you have the model of Romeo and Juliet or Cinderella and Prince Charming. In this model, the lovers find love at first sight, and the dramatic tension comes from external factors that conspire to keep them apart. On the other hand, you have the model of Belle and the Beast in *Beauty and the Beast*, or Benedick and Beatrice in *Much Ado about Nothing*. In this model, the two central characters hate each other at first, but gradually overcome their mutual dislike and grow into love.

The love story that we encounter in the Song of Songs belongs to the first variety. In our previous study, we heard only from the woman. We listened to her initial passionate outpouring of desire for the man, but at that point we had no indication of how he felt concerning her. Was the desire mutual, or was it destined to be unrequited, like a teenage crush that dies unspoken and is later only an embarrassing memory?

In this episode, not only do we learn that her love is shared, but we see their mutual affection growing through their dialogue. This reminds us that love is not a hole in the ground into which you "fall," more or less by accident. Love is a relationship, and like all other relationships, it needs to be fed and nurtured if it is to grow into real intimacy. As wisdom literature, this passage provides us with guidance and encouragement from God that will challenge, convict, and direct us as we pursue our own romantic relationships. Yet the greatest love story of all—the true Song of Songs in our lives—is our relationship with the God who made us for himself. As a result, this passage also speaks to our relationship with God and our pursuit of intimacy with him.

Dark but Beautiful

The poem begins with the woman expressing her fear that she is unattractive because she doesn't fit the conventional stereotype of beauty in her culture. She is dark (Song 1:5), which here is not a racial feature but a social feature: it comes not from her birth and ethnicity but from having been forced to work outside in the vineyards, where the harsh glare of the sun has darkened her complexion. Yet at the same time, there is a note of defiance in her voice. She is dark, but she is nonetheless beautiful. Though she may appear like the dark, coarse material that the Bedouin tribes of Kedar used for their tents, she declares that she is still beautiful like the curtains of Solomon, the palace wall hangings that would have been the height of urban chic.

This opening statement marks her out as a peasant girl concerned about how she measures up against the daughters of Jerusalem, the attractive and refined city-dwellers. In ancient cultures, there would have been no market for tanning salons: the sign of being a wealthy woman was the ability to stay out of the sun. Poor people worked in the fields where their skin became darker and darker, while rich women stayed indoors and could keep their skin pale.[1] Indeed, in some countries this bias continues: on a recent trip to Sri Lanka, I saw a number of skin "brightening" and "lightening" products for sale. After the industrial revolution, however, when poor people grew pale from working in factories for sixteen hours a day, the rich had to find a new way to distinguish themselves, and the concept of a "healthy tan" was born.

The woman not only is from a poor background but also comes from a difficult family situation. Her father is never mentioned in the Song, and her relatives are not described here as her brothers but "the sons of my mother," which is a more distant relational term (Song 1:6). She has no one to protect and provide for her, but is forced by her family to work in the vineyards in the burning heat of the Middle Eastern sun. At the same time, she has not been able to maintain her own "vineyard," that is, her body. She hasn't been able to devote the necessary time and resources to developing her own appearance as she would like. She feels like Cinderella, exploited and oppressed as a servant in her own home, waiting for her prince to come and carry her off to a new life of abundance and affection.

1. Anthropologist Marvin Harris studied the historical use of parasols, and he observed that royalty and wealthy "nobles" from Rome to northern Africa were seen being shaded from the effects of the sun with celebratory umbrellas and parasols, while common people were forbidden from using such devices. This was connected to pallid skin being seen as a marker of upper-class status. See Kerry Segrave, *Suntanning in 20th Century America* (Jefferson, NC: McFarland & Company, 2005), 8.

Where Are You?

Having defiantly affirmed her beauty in spite of many external difficulties, the woman asks her beloved to give her directions so that she can find him. Whereas earlier she described the man as a king, now he is a shepherd, working out in the field with his flocks (Song 1:7). As so often in poetry, the poet here uses a dazzling kaleidoscope of metaphors to communicate his meaning. These are not completely unrelated metaphors, since in antiquity (as well as in the Bible) kings were often described as the shepherds of their people, tasked with caring for them and watching over them. Yet no reigning king or member of the royal family would literally have been employed as a shepherd facing the dangers and discomforts of life out in the fields. Royalty had servants to undertake such menial tasks. Nor is the focus of the metaphor here on the shepherd's role in caring for his flock but rather on the opportunities and challenges that such a lifestyle presents for the couple in building a relationship. How can she find him, when he is moving from place to place?

The woman's love is such that she cannot simply wait for him to come home at the end of the day: she wants to be with him at noon as well. At that time of day, the flocks would generally be lying down rather than moving around; yet to be outside with her beloved means further exposure to the harsh gaze of the sun (see Song 1:6). It also means being exposed to social risks: she fears being viewed as a veiled woman by his fellow shepherds (v. 7). Those who wore veils and wandered around among the shepherds typically were not women of good reputation: they were usually prostitutes, as Tamar pretended to be in Genesis 38. Yet the woman is willing to take that risk to her reputation, if she can only find him and be with him.

Here I Am

The man's response is immediately encouraging and sensitive to her concerns. He begins by calling her "most beautiful of women" and giving her directions to find him, thereby answering both of her concerns (Song 1:8). In fact, his teasing tone suggests that she ought to know exactly where to find him: she should just follow the trail that he has left for her. He isn't playing hard to get. Moreover, the man compares her to a mare among Pharaoh's chariots (v. 9). Many commentators see this as a reference to the ancient military tactic of releasing a mare in heat onto the battlefield in an attempt to create havoc among the enemy stallions pulling the chariots. The focus of the passage, however, seems to be on decoration rather than pheromones: the point of the comparison is rather that she is like one of the highly decorated royal horses known from both Egypt and Persia.[2] Just as those pampered royal horses wore decorated bridles, so her cheeks were adorned with gold and silver earrings and her neck with a necklace (or perhaps an Egyptian-style collar) of jewels.

The woman responds to the man's affirming words with a renewed expression of her own desire for him, in three verses that are linked by the theme of fragrance and connect back to her initial words of desire in Song 1:2–4. She once again calls the man her "king," as in verse 4; but whereas in verse 3 she delighted in *his* scent, now she wishes for *her* scent to come to him as he reclines on his couch, perhaps eating a meal with friends (v. 12). The woman longs for the distance between them, which is maintained throughout this section, to be bridged. Instead of her scent merely wafting over to him on a distant couch, she wants him to be as close to her as physically possible. She wishes that he were like a sprig of myrrh resting between her breasts all night long (v. 13). She compares her beloved to a cluster of henna in the vineyards of Engedi, an oasislike setting on the shores of the Dead Sea, known for its royal vineyards and gardens (v. 14). In contrast to the arid wilderness setting all around, her beloved is like a fragrant flower in the midst of a garden.

Evaluating Beauty

So how does this poem address our longing for love? In the first place, it openly acknowledges our deep insecurity. When the woman declares, "I am dark but beautiful," she is crying out for affirmation. She wants someone to see her and love her just as she is, complete with her weather-beaten complexion, complicated family situation, and everything that goes into being her. The fashions in feminine beauty may have shifted, but concerns over appearance and body image continue to plague us.[3] Now we no longer

2. See Steven Horine, *Interpretive Images in the Song of Songs: From Wedding Chariots to Bridal Chambers* (New York: Peter Lang, 2001), 134.

3. See Shannon Hodde Miller, "'Am I Pretty?' A Troubling Question among Christian Women like Me," *CT* (March 9, 2012), http://www.christianitytoday.com/women/2012/march/am-i-pretty-troubling-question-among-christian-women-like.html?paging=off.

praise a woman with a pale complexion and a "traditionally built,"[4] robust figure but instead admire those who are tanned and stick-thin. In our culture, there is more pressure on men also to look just right, with their shirts on or off. We live in a culture that adulates external beauty and takes the pursuit of the appearance of "health," as we euphemistically call our idolatry, to unhealthy extremes.

We certainly bring that cultural concern into our pursuit of romantic relationships. We quickly judge people on the basis of body type or hair color, dismissing as unsuitable anyone who doesn't quite fit the standard. No one "dark" need apply. That concern with outward appearance may be quite revealing about what we are seeking in a relationship: we want someone attractive to be with us because that makes us feel good about ourselves. It affirms us and answers our own insecurities: if I can get someone attractive to be interested in me, then I am a significant person. The Song invites us to open our eyes and see beyond the cultural stereotypes of beauty to love people for who they are, not just for their outward appearance.

In many church contexts, unfortunately, our evaluation of one another is no different from that of the world around us. Anyone who doesn't fit the cultural stereotype of beauty is a second-class citizen. Added to that problem is the Christian perfectionist streak in our pursuit of spouses that finds little room for the possibility that someone could be "dark but beautiful." We affirm a gospel that declares us all broken but loved, and say that we are seeking someone who will love us with our own very real flaws, but at the same time, we often shy away from pursuing anyone with a complicated personal history. Again, the problem often lies in our heart idolatries and our selfishness. We are looking for a marriage partner who will make us look good, rather than a fellow sinner to love and to serve.

Complicating matters further, some of us wrestle with the opposite idolatry, being drawn to deeply broken people because we want to be their savior, the knight in shining armor who fixes their problems. We forget that the person we marry may also be the mother or father of our children. There is nothing intrinsically better in being drawn to someone with deep problems.

4. The phrase comes from Alexander McCall Smith's The No. 1 Ladies' Detective Agency series of books, set in Botswana.

History matters: a person's past is not simply airbrushed away at the point of conversion. Some people will continue to need a great deal of emotional and spiritual support throughout their Christian lives. Yet the "dark but beautiful" image suggests that we should be open to relationships with people who have great struggles in their lives if we see those struggles beginning to produce godly fruit and grow them toward spiritual maturity. Trajectory matters even more than history.

After all, if the first quality we are looking for in a potential spouse is a love for the gospel, then some of the best marriage candidates will not have a squeaky-clean past. Instead, they will have a deep love for God that is forged out of the experience of their own sinfulness. As Jesus pointed out, the person who has been forgiven much loves much (Luke 7:47). Perhaps, therefore, instead of instantly discarding the boyfriend who confesses his struggles with Internet pornography, a Christian woman should be open to the possibility that here is someone who is actually willing to be honest and open about his problems. Perhaps the person who wrestles with same-sex attraction in a godly way is worth taking the time to get to know as a potential marriage partner. We should be looking for someone whose own darkness ignites in him or her a deep love for the beauty of Christ.

Affirmation

More precisely, the Song reminds us that what is truly important is not some "objective" measure of our attractiveness but the fact that we *feel* beautiful to the one who loves us. The woman's original statement is made to the daughters of Jerusalem, the sophisticated city-dwellers who surround her, whose gaze she fears will be as harsh and wounding as the summer sun (Song 1:5–6). Yet we never get to hear what they think of her. We don't find out whether the daughters of Jerusalem's verdict on her is "Too dark," "Gorgeously exotic!," or "Has potential given a proper makeover." At the end of the day, it doesn't matter whether an ancient fashionista thinks that this woman can make it as Jerusalem's next top model. What matters is what her lover thinks of her: to him, she is the most beautiful of women. The man doesn't dismiss her fears over her appearance as unspiritual or ridiculous. Instead, he responds to them kindly with words that repeatedly affirm her beauty, as well as seeking to enhance it with gifts of jewelry. Through his words of affirmation and praise, he builds her up and assures her of his love in precisely the area where she feels most unlovely.

This kind of care is typical, ideally, of the early stages of a relationship. As we noted earlier, during the infatuation phase of a relationship, lovers loudly sing each other's praises. That is as it should be: on your wedding day, you should be able to celebrate the glorious beauty of the person to whom you are devoting the rest of your life. It is not enough to know that this person is a Christian and that your families tell you that you are good together. It is not enough to marry someone because you are not sure that anyone better will come along. Attraction matters! Of course, attraction is a multifaceted thing. We are drawn toward and fall in love with whole people, not just bodies. We may be drawn toward a person's sparkling personality, or his compassionate care for others, or her zany sense of humor—virtues that more than compensate for what others see as major flaws in appearance. What is more, the person you marry will not be perfect, and before you marry you should have a clear idea of the person's flaws and characteristic sins. There are *in spite of*s as well as *because of*s in every relationship. But even though you may know that she is never likely to grace the cover of *Vogue*, or that he is not likely to be voted one of this year's 100 sexiest men, you should still be able to describe your spouse as "most beautiful of women" or "most attractive of men," because to you that is exactly what she or he is.

Nor should you cease speaking such words of affirmation after you get married. Words of affirmation have tremendous power in any relationship, and no one else shapes your view of yourself more than your spouse. If your spouse says that you are beautiful and successful, then you will feel beautiful and successful. On the other hand, if your spouse repeatedly tears you down and mocks you, it will create a void in your soul that no amount of external success or adulation of others can fill. This was the way that God intended it to be in the beginning: two people who become one flesh, united in outlook, building each other up with words that encourage and affirm. But when a body is destroying itself and tearing itself apart, it is a devastating problem. We instinctively know that when people harm their bodies through self-mutilation or cutting, something is seriously wrong. Yet what you say to your spouse about his or her appearance or attractiveness matters just as deeply, even if you claim that it is "only a joke."

Pursuing Intimacy

The woman doesn't simply want to be admired and praised for her appearance as if she were a life-size doll, however. She longs for real intimacy with her beloved, an intimacy that bridges the gap between human beings. She wants to be with him about his work during the day and to have him sleep in her arms all night long. The Bible tells us that it is not good for a man to be alone (Gen. 2:18), and the same is true for women as well. We were not made to live alone but to pursue intimacy with one another. Although God has given some people the gift of singleness as a vocation, most people are called to find their deepest intimacy through the relationship of marriage.

Again, this is countercultural. We live in a wider culture that puts marriage on the back burner, deferring it until after our other goals—especially our educational and career goals—have been achieved. We say, "Once I complete graduate school and get established in my field, then I'll think about marriage." Yet our desire for intimacy, both physical and relational, doesn't go away. As a result, we may find ourselves engaging in a string of emotional and sexual affairs in the meantime. Sociologist Mark Regnerus comments:

> Time and again, I've listened to Christian undergraduates recount to me how their relationships turned sexual. One thing I never ask them is *why*. I know why. Because sex feels great, it feels connectional, it feels deeply human. I never blame them for wanting that. Sex is intended to deepen personal relationships, and desire for it is intended to promote marriage.[5]

By deferring marriage indefinitely, we set ourselves up for failure: we were made for the intimacy of marriage, and in the absence of the reality it should not be surprising that the counterfeits seem irresistibly attractive. In the Song, the woman is willing to exert considerable effort and take social risks in order to pursue this intimacy. It is the primary goal in her life. She is willing to go out in the heat of the day, when, according to Noel Coward's song, all but mad dogs and Englishmen normally stay home. She is willing to risk misunderstanding and abuse on the part of the shepherds. She just

5. Mark Regnerus, "The Case for Early Marriage," *CT* (July 31, 2009), http://www.christianitytoday.com/ct/2009/august/16.22.html.

longs to be with her beloved. He in turn responds to her efforts, enabling her to find her way to him. Real relationships are built on this kind of intimacy, which takes time and effort and the willingness to take risks.

Idolizing Marriage

Yet in a fallen world, such intimacy is hard to find, even within marriage. If the wider culture (along with some Christians) has ignored or denigrated marriage as unnecessary, or something that can easily be deferred to a more suitable time of life, the church in our day and age has sometimes so idolized marriage that it feels as though you are incomplete and a failure if you are unmarried, or if your marriage is anything less than a bed of roses. The reality of the world in which we live is that some men and women have not yet found their "king"—a person with whom they can share a lifelong love story. Others have found marriage, but not the intimacy that marriage was supposed to bring. There are people who are lonelier in their marriages than they ever were as singles. In the face of such marital difficulties, some people merely plod through life, existing rather than living, while others have abandoned disappointing marriages in pursuit of the deceptive mirage of extramarital intimacy. Still others have lost faithful spouses to death, or have been abandoned by those who promised their hearts to them. For many, marriage is a dry and barren wasteland rather than a land flowing with milk and honey.

In that context, where so many bear the scars of past relationships, it is easy for us to pursue intimacy in all the wrong places. We may seek it through the fake form of pornography or romantic literature, or through serial sexual relationships, in an attempt to fill our inner void. In this case, we pursue our disordered or disappointed desire for intimacy with a passion. Alternatively, we may grow hard and cynical, protecting our hearts against damage by hiding them away, refusing to risk pursuing intimacy when we have been disappointed so many times before. On this approach, we deal with our disordered desire for intimacy by denying it and stuffing it away.

Finding Intimacy

With its utopian enthusiasm, the Song reminds us that our desire for intimacy is fundamentally a good desire. Deep down, we all long for what the woman in the Song desires: someone who finds her beautiful, in spite of her dark skin; someone who will affirm her, even though the difficulties that she has experienced within her family have left her vineyard uncultivated and unkempt. Oh, to be loved by someone who will love us like that!

Is such love even possible to hope for? Yes, it is. This poem serves as a powerful antidote to the cynicism that so easily invades our wounded hearts. It wafts the scent of henna blossoms under our noses, encouraging us to remember that there is a fragrant oasis in the desert of life. Intimacy is not an impossible dream after which we strive in vain. There is hope of bridging the gap that separates us as men and women.

For some, that rich intimacy will indeed be found in marriage—not perfectly, but truly. Whether it is love at first sight or a relationship that starts out badly and then somehow turns around, true love exists and is a rich blessing. If God has given you that kind of relationship with a spouse, give him thanks for his good gift and fight hard for the kind of intimacy that the Song celebrates. Affirm and celebrate each other's one-of-a-kind beauty and gifting. Delight in the ways in which your beloved is unique, and take the time to express that appreciation to him or her. Pursue each other in the heat of the day and in the cool of the evening, with a fervent and passionate commitment to love, cherish, and serve each other, laying down your life daily for your spouse.

For others, life is not like that. God has not given you an intimate marriage, or perhaps he has not given you a marriage at all. Are you therefore consigned to a less-than-human existence, thirsting for an intimacy that you will never find in this life? Not at all. After all, Jesus—the most perfect human who ever existed—never experienced marriage or sexual intimacy but nonetheless had deep and joyful relationships with his twelve disciples and other friends, both men and women, as well as with his heavenly Father. This shows us that we can find deep and true intimacy by pursuing rich friendships with people of our own gender, relationships that we often neglect in our desperate desire to be married. In the church, God has given us a family: brothers and sisters who can love us just as we are, recognizing our darkness and celebrating our beauty, affirming our unique gifting. The church is intended to be a place of deep intimacy, of being known and loved just as we are, for the sake of Jesus Christ.

Of course, if this kind of intimacy is going to happen in the church, we will need to pursue it with effort and eagerness, as well as with grace and forgiveness toward others who often fail us and let us down. You can't develop an intimate relationship with people whom you see for only a couple of hours on Sunday morning. This is where community groups and ministry teams come in. They create the context in which deep and intimate relationships may be formed, in which people can rejoice with us when we rejoice and weep with us when we weep. Whether God has given you a great marriage or not, you are called to find and give encouragement, affirmation, and intimacy through a rich web of relationships in the church.

Intimacy with God

Yet even the church will often let us down and disappoint us. Even in the best marriage and the best church, our longings for sexual and relational intimacy never find complete fulfillment in this broken world. The richest and deepest hope of intimacy is not to be found in any merely human relationship. Whether you are deeply bonded to others or a loner, whether you are married or unmarried, true intimacy is ultimately to be found only in the One who loved us before the world began, Jesus Christ. Our desire for human intimacy, our longing to be known and loved deeply by someone who knows everything about us and loves us anyway, is a reflex of our desire for intimacy with our Creator.

The truth is that we are all deeply scarred by our genetics and our circumstances. We are dark people, who are damaged not merely by our environment and the effects of the sun's rays, but by multitudinous forms of our own personal sin and idolatry. We long to be beautiful, but we know deep down that we are not. We have not kept our vineyard. Later on in the Song, the woman delights to give her vineyard, which represents her body, joyfully and uniquely to her husband (Song 8:12). Sadly, many of us have not protected our purity in this way; instead, we have left the gate of our vineyard open and its walls unguarded. Others may technically be virgins, according to the school of lexical semantics in which what counts as having sex with someone is rather narrowly defined. Yet when we measure ourselves against the standard of Jesus in the Sermon on the Mount, all of us are defiled by our lust (Matt. 5:27–28); none of us have kept the vineyard of our minds pure and above reproach.

Some of us also share the woman's story of a complicated relationship with our families, perhaps even experiencing abuse from the very people who should have protected us. As a result, our sexual responses are confused. We seem programmed toward same-sex attraction, perhaps, or away from any sexual interaction at all. This can make it seem risky to pursue rich relationships with people of the same gender, in the face of battling sexual attraction, or any relationships at all, given our history of abuse. What hope is there for scarred and broken people like us to find true intimacy with the God who reveals himself in blinding holiness and majesty?

Our Shepherd-King

We find the answer in the One who is both our King and our Shepherd, Jesus Christ. Instead of waiting for us to come out in the heat of the day looking for him, our Shepherd came searching for us. Jesus bore both ridicule and abuse in his pursuit of his beloved, as he entered the wilderness of this world seeking to find and to save us—those who were utterly lost. He left behind the perfect intimacy that he had enjoyed with the Father from all eternity, so that he could give us an intimacy with him that we had despised and lost through our own sin, an intimacy that we never even knew that we needed or wanted. In order to win that intimate relationship with us, the Father bruised and disfigured his own beloved Son on the cross to pay for our sins. Jesus had no beauty or majesty in his appearance to draw people to him to begin with, but in that climactic moment of history, he was marred beyond comprehension (see Isa. 53). At the cross, the light , fellowship was turned away, and the deepest and coldest darkness of the soul enveloped the Son as he took our darkness into himself. Through that sacrifice, though, Jesus now clothes us in glorious royal robes of his righteousness, adorning us with a breathtaking beauty that we do not merit and could not earn. Our blackness is dealt with once and for all, swallowed up in his beauty: now the glorious light of the Father's countenance shines on us forever.

This is the remedy for all our faltering and failed attempts to find intimacy with one another. The very best of husbands and wives have sinned many times against their spouses and have not loved them as they should. All of us, whether single or married, have repeatedly failed to pursue God and those around us with purity, choosing instead to pursue the easy false intimacy offered by our idols. Yet our Beloved still invites us out of our thirsty lives in the wilderness into the oasis of his love. He calls us his "most beautiful" and welcomes us to share profound intimacy with him. Jesus knows everything about us, including the deepest, darkest secrets that we have shared with no one else on earth. Yet he still loves us and wants to spend eternity with us. Here is the true intimacy and love for which we all long.

Is this Redeemer your Beloved? The story of our relationship with God is neither love at first sight nor a mutual hatred that is gradually transformed. Instead, it is a story of God's unchanging love for his own, and our utterly unreasonable hatred of him. He calls us to come to him just as we are, but we refuse to acknowledge him for who he is, the Creator and Sovereign Lord of the universe. We try to remake him into a more comfortable deity, a god who will serve us and do our bidding, instead of vice versa. Salvation comes to us, though, when we give up our attempts to remake God in our image and instead bow our hearts before him in submission, opening ourselves to receive his Holy Spirit and to begin to be changed into the image of Christ. Our hearts are warmed as we contemplate the gospel: the more we see God's love to us at the cross, the easier it will be for us to bow before the aspects of his wisdom that we find hard to understand and accept. Has that transformation begun in you, as you cease your resistance to Christ and submit to his loving entreaty to come and receive life from him?

If you have begun such a transformation, are you allowing God's evaluation of you to shape your thinking, not the evaluation of your idols all around you? If he calls you beautiful, in spite of your continuing brokenness, are you not beautiful indeed? No matter what others say about you, or what the voices in your head say about you, if Jesus Christ the Crucified calls you his beloved, then that is what you really are. You have been loved by an everlasting love: you are his and he is yours, embraced by a love that will not let you go. Today and every day, let that reality direct your thinking, giving you a joy that no sorrow or loss on earth can snatch from you and a peace that no trial can destroy. When your blackness presses in upon you, let this be your refuge. Heaven and earth may fade and flee away, but you can know this: while you and God exist, you are his and he is yours—forever.[6]

6. See George W. Robinson's hymn "Loved with Everlasting Love" (1876).

3

Crazy Love

Song of Songs 1:15—2:7

Man
15 Behold! You are beautiful, my darling!
Behold! You are beautiful!
Your eyes are doves!

Woman
16 Behold! You are beautiful, my beloved!
How lovely! How verdant is our bed!
17 The beams of our house are cedars;
our rafters are pine trees.

2:1 I am [just] a wildflower of Sharon, a lily of the valleys.

Man
2 Like a lily among brambles
is my darling among young women.

Woman
3 Like an apple tree among the trees of the forest,
so is my beloved among the young men.
With great delight, I sit in his shade,
and his fruit is sweet in my mouth,

4 He brought me to the house of wine,
and his banner over me was love.
5 Prepare for me a bed with raisin cakes;
stretch me out among apples,
for I am weak with love.
6 May his left hand be under my head,
and his right hand embrace me!
7 I charge you, daughters of Jerusalem,
by the gazelles or the does of the field,
that you will not arouse or awaken love
until it delights.

This saying is often attributed to Sigmund Freud: "One is very crazy when in love." Being Freud, what he actually said was: "The state of being in love which is psychologically so remarkable . . . is the normal prototype of the psychoses."[1] What I think he meant by that, however, was this: "Being in love is very much like being crazy!" You obsess over another person and engage in highly embarrassing forms of speech that would otherwise never cross your lips. You rearrange your whole life simply to manufacture opportunities for "chance" encounters. Shortly after the beginning of our relationship in Africa, my wife, Barb, sent a letter home to her parents in America consisting of an entire page that simply read, "I'm in love! I'm in love! I'm in love! . . ." Likewise, when I went on a trip to do some electrical work at a remote mission station, I arranged to have a note delivered to her mailbox *every single day* while I was gone. Definitely crazy.

Rhapsody in Words

We get a sense of that craziness in the opening conversation between the man and the woman in this passage: "Wow![2] You are beautiful!" he says. To which she replies in almost identical words. Here is a couple who are completely enraptured with each other. His attention is focused on her eyes,

1. Sigmund Freud, *Totem and Taboo* (London: Routledge, 1950), 104.

2. *Hinneh* in Hebrew often expresses surprise and wonder, and it is traditionally translated as "Behold!" In more contemporary speech, however, we would be more likely to say something such as "Wow!"

which he compares to doves (Song 1:15). He will repeat the same comparison at the beginning of chapter 4 as the introduction to a much longer description of her appearance (4:1–7). It's not exactly clear how her eyes remind him of doves. Is it their shape? Their color? Their liveliness? Perhaps not every metaphor in poetry is precisely analyzable. In this case, it may be more significant that he is captivated by her eyes, which are so powerful in communicating a person's thoughts. Like Rachel before her (Gen. 29:17), this woman has eyes that are the key to her beauty. Indeed, gazing into someone's eyes is surely one of the most powerfully personal and intimate experiences that there is.

The woman is equally captivated by the man, but her praise moves in a different direction. She describes their bed as "verdant" (Song 1:16)—that is, green and growing prolifically like a lush garden—and their house as being constructed out of cedars and pine trees. For some reason, many commentators seem to imagine that this poem speaks of the woman's desire for sex in the woods,[3] but that surely misses the metaphor here. When the woman describes their bed as being green, she doesn't have simply sex on her mind, but fertility—abundant offspring. Like any normal ancient Near Eastern woman, she is thinking about bearing his children. Likewise, when she speaks of their "house" (v. 17), the woman is imagining the family that they will construct together, built out of solid and lasting materials, like pine and cedar. Don't miss the crucial pronoun *our* as well. Previously, she spoke of wanting to be in *his* chambers and *his* couch. Now that he has spoken of his love for her, though, she is starting to think about the home that they will build together.

This is the classic language of love at all times and places, as the man and the woman fantasize about a lasting, committed, and intimate relationship together. It is an oddity of our place and time that we have so disconnected sex from marriage and family that it has been reduced to a mere experience in its own right. Historically speaking, it is entirely normal not merely to want to gaze into each other's eyes but to raise a family together, and for sexual desire to fit within that bigger picture.

In the next section, the man and the woman continue to express their mutual affirmation of each other. Rather self-deprecatingly, she calls herself

3. E.g., Tremper Longman III, *Song of Songs*, NICOT (Grand Rapids: Eerdmans, 2001), 108.

"just" a wildflower[4] of Sharon, an ordinary lily[5] among the thousands that dot the valleys (Song 2:1). The man responds by turning her description around. She may be a lily, but she is not just a lily among other lilies. Rather, she is a lily among thorns (v. 2)—a unique beauty in a world of ugly and unproductive weeds.

The woman returns the compliment by calling the man an apple tree among the trees of the forest (Song 2:3). He is uniquely attractive in a world of men that to her are otherwise all the same. She unfolds the comparison in terms of two specific attributes: she delights to sit in his shade and eat his fruit. Some commentators have also interpreted these words as having a sexual reference, but although there are plenty of places in the Song of Songs where the lovers are talking about sex, I don't think this is one of them. The metaphor seems straightforward enough as it stands. When she says that she delights to sit in his shade and eat his fruit, she is simply declaring that she revels in his protection of and provision for her.

Beautifully Different

What is important here are the similarities and differences in the compliments that they pay each other. Each has affirming words to say about the other, building the other person up rather than tearing down. As we discussed in the previous chapter, this pattern of mutual affirmation and respect is tremendously important in a healthy marriage. Yet what is equally striking in this passage is that, having begun with almost identical words of praise, the content of their affirmation diverges in ways that reveal fundamental differences between the man and the woman. He loves her beautiful eyes, which are the windows of her soul. She compares him to a tree in whose shade she longs to sit and whose fruit she delights to eat. Later on, we will see that she will also compare his eyes to doves (Song 5:12), and he will compare her to a tree whose fruit he wants to taste (7:7–9). Yet the similarities also

4. The traditional English translation that identifies her as a "rose" is not supported by the Hebrew. As can be seen from Isaiah 35:1, the bloom in question is clearly a common desert wildflower, perhaps an asphodel or a crocus.

5. Although the Hebrew word *šôšānnâ* is rendered as "lily" by most English translations, many scholars have argued that it should more accurately be identified as a "lotus," which is a kind of water lily. Given the "exotic" overtones of lotus flowers in our culture compared to the "homeliness" of lilies, however, I think that the traditional translation perhaps better captures the poetic connotations of the word. It also allows the apt comparison with Jesus' use of the word in Matthew 6:28.

reveal profound differences: he is like an apple tree, in whose shade she longs to sit, while she is like a palm tree that he longs to climb so that he can lay hold of its dates.

These related but different metaphors invite us to consider the similarities and differences between men and women in relationships. There are real differences between the genders that are not simply the product of our culture and environment. Men and women were made by God to be interdependent but not interchangeable, and part of that difference is that the man is intended by God to protect and provide for the woman. As Matthew Henry beautifully put it, Eve was "not made out of [Adam's] head to rule over him, nor out of his feet to be trampled upon by him, but out of his side to be equal with him, under his arm to be protected, and near his heart to be beloved."[6]

Of course, not all men are the same, and neither are all women, and different cultures view their tasks differently as well. There is room for all kinds of diversity of temperament, gifting, and calling: protecting and providing for your wife does not necessarily mean going out into the forest and dragging home a dead deer at the end of the day, while godly womanhood does not necessarily involve spending your time baking cakes and arranging flowers. In some contexts, the husband may protect and provide for his family by orchestrating a stable home environment that allows the wife to use her gifts in the workplace. Yet there is nonetheless a God-given role for men of protecting and providing, of leading and laying down their lives for their brides, in a relationship that is not simply reversible.

In the next image, the woman pictures the two of them in a "house of wine," where she sits under his banner of love (Song 2:4). On one level, a house of wine is simply a private place where the man and the woman can feast and enjoy intimacy together. On another level, it evokes the earlier metaphor that the woman used when she described his kisses and caresses as better than wine. Meanwhile, banners in the Old Testament were clan and military markers: she has left her parental clan and now joyfully places herself under her beloved's banner, submitting herself to his authority. Again, it is significant that the woman sits under the banner of his authority, not vice versa. Yet her submission is not a chore or an enforced and resentful act, for to be in his presence is a feast, and his banner of authority is emblazoned with his

6. Matthew Henry, *Matthew Henry's Commentary* (Peabody, MA: Hendrickson, 1991), 1:16.

love for her. Who would not joyfully submit to such a caring shepherd-king? Here we see a poetic description of the biblical model of male headship: sensitive, loving, self-sacrificial leadership that doesn't squash women but creates a freeing framework for them to flourish in their God-given roles.

Longing for Consummation

Yet while this consummation of their feast is so eagerly desired, it is as yet only a future dream. She longs for the day when his left hand will be under her head and his right hand will embrace her (Song 2:6). In the meantime, however, until that day of consummation and satisfaction comes, she is weak and sick with love (v. 5). In ancient Near Eastern love poetry, people are never lovesick in the presence of their beloveds—only in their absence.[7] Here the woman needs to lie down and be nourished in the meantime with apples and raisin cakes, sweet and celebratory foods that will remind her of their love and sustain her until the day when that love can finally be consummated.

Out of her experience of the crazy joy and heartrending frustration of love, she then speaks words of counsel to the daughters of Jerusalem, charging them on oath not to stir up or arouse love until its proper time (Song 2:7). This refrain will recur twice more in the Song (3:5; 8:4), marking it out as an important part of the Song's message. God has created us in such a way that love is powerful; sexual passion is powerful. It is not something to be toyed with. Yet neither is love or sex something to be denigrated or denied because it is somehow dirty or unspiritual. There is a proper time for love and sexual passion, a time when it will be appropriate and right to release its overwhelming power. Until that proper time comes, however, it is something to wait for, not to rush into.

One strange aspect of the oath is the fact that the woman charges the daughters of Jerusalem by the gazelles and the does of the field not to stir up love. Now, if you think it a little odd to make someone swear an oath by some deer, you are right. But there is an untranslatable play on words here. On the one hand, as we will see, gazelles and does are associated with love throughout the Song. In a sense, the daughters of Jerusalem are thus being asked to swear their oath by love itself. On the other hand, the word

7. Michael V. Fox, *The Song of Songs and the Ancient Egyptian Love Songs* (Madison, WI: University of Wisconsin Press, 1985), 109.

gazelles in Hebrew sounds identical to the word *Hosts* in the title *Lord of Hosts*, and the phrase *does of the field* sounds very similar to *God Almighty*. These wordplays leave little doubt as to who the true God of love is, by whom they are to swear.[8]

The Virtues and Dangers of Crazy Love

So how does this poem speak to our own human relationships? Crazy love is not a major theme elsewhere in the Old Testament. There are depictions of some good marriage relationships: for example, Boaz and Ruth, and Rebekah in her willingness to leave home and family by faith to marry a man she has never met, simply on the strength of God's promise (Gen. 24). Wise Abigail seems like a good catch for David after the death of her first husband, the fool Nabal (1 Sam. 25). Yet there are remarkably few passionate marriages in the Bible. To be sure, Jacob is obsessed by Rachel's beauty, so much so that he ends up working fourteen years for her (Gen. 29), but that hardly guarantees a happy home life for him. Even Boaz and Ruth's relationship seems to have more to do with Ruth's covenant loyalty (*hesed*, Ruth 3:10) to Naomi and her dead husband than it does with love (*'ahavah*). If all that we had were these historical examples, we might be inclined to conclude that everything the Bible needs to say on the subject of attraction is contained in Proverbs 31:30: "Charm is deceitful, and beauty is vain, but a woman who fears the Lord is to be praised." If that were the first and last word on the subject, our marriage counsel might be simplified to: "Find any good Christian of the opposite gender who is willing and available, and marry that person."

Of course, that is part of biblical wisdom on the subject, and it may be the part that some people most need to hear. In the context in which we live, some rank chemistry and appearance far too highly in what they are looking for in a partner, and as a result, they either are drawn toward totally unsuitable people by their outward attractiveness or pass over good candidates for marriage simply because they do not match the image that they have in mind. Because we are fallen people, we are often attracted by all the wrong things. There are many Christians who need to memorize Proverbs 31:30 and heed its counsel. Yet the Song of Songs is part of biblical wisdom as

8. Ibid., 110.

well, and it reminds us that there is another dimension to marriage. Strikingly, coming from a culture in which marriages would mostly have been arranged rather than chosen, it celebrates the craziness of love, the kind of love that knocks you out of your comfortable equilibrium and takes your breath away. Married love is not simply a matter of finding someone with whom to do the dishes. It is, as the Song will remind us later, a relationship on fire.

Full-orbed biblical wisdom thus challenges both traditional cultures, in which marriage is simply a matter of practical provision and not love, and modern Western culture, in which intense and passionate feelings are highly valued but often entirely disconnected from marriage. The Song of Songs reminds us that the exclusive, lifelong relationship of marriage is not supposed to be the opposite of such crazy love but its ideal vehicle. The pursuit of love and marriage are not two separate and opposite things but are intended to be one and the same: the dazzling, dizzying pursuit of a unique individual that results in a lifelong friendship in which you gaze deeply into each other's eyes *and* build a solid and lasting home and family together. That doesn't mean that every day in marriage is going to be like the first flush of infatuation. As C. S. Lewis pointed out, "Who could bear to live in that excitement for even five years? What would become of your work, your appetite, your sleep, your friendships?"[9] No one could survive at that constant level of passion. Nonetheless, in a good marriage you circle around repeatedly into recognizing afresh and celebrating the wonder of the person whom God has given you.

All of this explains why love is not something to be casually rushed into and stirred up. The dazzling, dizzying feelings of infatuation are intoxicating and confusing, like a drug. Indeed, in our culture it is a legal high that we routinely press upon teens and preteens, to the point at which thirteen-year-old middle-school students are expected to take dates to proms, where they will slow-dance together. Recreational dating, which we could define as forming an exclusive attachment to a member of the opposite sex whom you have absolutely no intention of marrying, has become the norm for many. Like all drugs, it feels good. Yet this kind of uncommitted pursuit of the opposite sex can inflict emotional scars, and easily leads to inappropriate sexual activity.

9. C. S. Lewis, *Mere Christianity* (London: G. Bles, 1969), 86.

The Pursuit of Marriage

Nor, on the other hand, is love and marriage to be inordinately delayed. Notice that the woman does not tell you not to stir up love until *you* are ready but until *it* is ready. This is not a process of which you are entirely in control, so that you can put love and marriage off until a convenient time for your plan for your life or until you feel totally prepared. The obverse of this counsel is Paul's advice to the Corinthians that it is better to marry than remain single and burn with passion (1 Cor. 7:9). If God has not given you the gift of singleness, then make marriage a serious pursuit. Men, look for a wife into whose eyes you can gaze and with whom you will build a stable Christian home and family. Women, look for a man who can protect and provide for you, under whose loving banner you will delight to sit.

We have a hard time getting the balance right between career and family. Biblically, both are admirable pursuits. Proverbs 22:29 tells us that a man who is skillful in his work will serve kings, not obscure men. There is an appropriate honor in a job well done. Yet at the same time, Proverbs 18:22 tells us that he who finds a wife finds a good thing and obtains favor from the Lord. Marriage is a real blessing—and parenting is a full-time and fulfilling career choice. Our problem is that we often pursue both career and family as a means to satisfy our own idolatries rather than seeing them as a calling from God to serve others. Our search for marriage should be at least as thoughtful and diligent as our search for a job.

To be sure, the search for marriage can be intensely frustrating precisely because love is not within your power to control. We can't schedule meeting Mr. or Miss Right and falling in love. In fact, this may be *the* key area of your life where God is at work, teaching you to be patient and to trust that he has something better than you can ask or imagine, and that you need to hurry up and wait, instead of trying to work out a relationship that everyone around you can see is unhealthy. Your goal, after all, is not just to get married but to have a good marriage, a marriage that is filled with the right kind of crazy love.

The intense driving power of sex inevitably makes our sexuality an area where the Holy Spirit will be at work sanctifying us, sometimes in unexpected ways. For those who struggle with same-sex attraction, it is an enormous spiritual challenge to wrestle with feelings that don't line up with what God's Word celebrates. Living with same-sex attraction is a difficult, humbling calling that needs to receive the encouragement and support of our brothers and sisters in Christ, as we seek together to follow the difficult path of obedience to God, rather than following our feelings. Others seem to be called by God to be single for a long time, even though they know that they don't have the gift of singleness. For these people, watching everyone around them pair off can be intensely painful. Every engagement party and baby shower can be another twist of the knife. Yet God often chooses such desert pathways to produce the sweet fruit of Christian maturity in his beloved children, and sometimes these saints will grow further in compassion, empathy, and the knowledge of God than others who lack their struggles. There may also be avenues of Christian service open to them that could never be pursued by married couples with children.

None of our human marriages can live up to the intimidating standard of the Song of Songs, though. Even the most happily married people you know will confess that their relationship is far from being filled with gazing deeply into each other's eyes every morning and writing love sonnets to each other every night. Life in a fallen world is hard, and so is marriage. Two sinners living together in a confined space gives plenty of opportunity for driving each other crazy rather than fulfilling each other's fantasies. Add in a pack of sinful children, and it is a recipe for mayhem. In God's design, however, it is also a sanctifying mayhem. Marriage is not the only sanctifying form of mayhem that God uses in our lives: for some, that sanctifying process comes through long-term singleness, or through the loss of a marriage relationship through death or divorce. God sanctifies each of his children in a unique way, giving each of them his or her own story. It is always tempting to long for the story that God wrote for someone else, whether that story is marriage, or a seemingly better marriage than ours, or even singleness. Yet God wrote your personal story with the goal of sanctifying you in exactly the ways he planned. This means that where you find yourself today—single, in a troubled marriage, or in a wonderful marriage—is exactly the place where you are supposed to be at this point in your story.

God's Crazy Love

The crazy passion that goes with marriage and sex—whether fulfilled or frustrated in our own story—is intended to give us a glimpse of an even crazier passion, which is the love that God has for his people. Did I say that there are few examples of crazy love in the Old Testament? There is one person in the Old Testament whose grand passion for his bride is truly dazzling and dizzying: the Lord. The Lord chose Israel to be his bride in the first place and set his love upon her. In Ezekiel 16, the Lord depicts his care for Jerusalem as being like a man who found an abandoned baby girl lying in a field beside the road, uncared-for and alone. The Lord took her in and tenderly gave her everything that she needed or wanted, dressing her in the finest clothing and adorning every part of her anatomy with jewels. Though Israel had no special beauty to draw the Lord to her—truly, she was just another wildflower in a field (see Ezek. 16:7)—he nonetheless chose her to be his unique bride. He was her shelter and her shade, her protector and provider, making sure that she lacked for nothing.

Yet the Lord's crazy love for his bride was not reciprocated. Instead, she abandoned her true and faithful Husband and went out and committed adultery with a variety of idols. Instead of maintaining the purity of their marriage bed, she sought fertility from Baal and Asherah under the verdant branches of the high places. Some of the cedar and pine that the Lord had provided to build a lasting house where he would dwell in their midst was used by Solomon to build houses for the gods of his foreign wives.

The book of Hosea fills in the rest of the story. In an acted-out parable, the Lord told his prophet to go and marry an adulterous and unfaithful woman, Gomer (Hos. 1–3). He told Hosea that Gomer would cheat on him, and that after she cheated on him, he should go after her again and woo her back, loving her and her illegitimate children in spite of the way that she had trampled on his affections. What kind of crazy love continues to pursue and to protect and to provide for someone who has been so completely unfaithful? The Lord's love does.

We never get to hear the end of Hosea and Gomer's story. Was Gomer's heart moved by his incredible compassion and love, or did she remain hardened toward him forever? We don't find out. But the end of the book of Hosea shows us the end of the Lord's love story with Israel in words that dramatically recall the language of this passage from the Song of Songs.[10] In the days to come, the Lord declares, Israel will blossom like a lily (Hos.

10. See Daniel C. Fredericks and Daniel J. Estes, *Ecclesiastes & the Song of Songs*, AOTC 16 (Downers Grove, IL: InterVarsity Press, 2010), 320.

14:5); she will return and sit under the Lord's shade (v. 7), and she will recognize that her fruit comes from him alone (v. 8). In other words, the Lord and his people will finally enjoy the kind of mutual relationship of crazy love and affection that exists between the woman and the man in the Song of Songs.

Let us bring this closer to home. For Israel is not the only one who has been gloriously loved by God and then proved spectacularly unfaithful. Gomer's story is not just Israel's story; it is our story, too. We have turned our backs on the God who gave us life and breath, choosing to pursue our idols instead. God has given us many good gifts—talents, opportunities, relationships, and possessions—and we have treated them as though they were our own and squandered them in service of other gods. Some of us have literally prostituted ourselves in pursuit of the dizzying, dazzling feelings that surround sex. Instead of viewing our sexuality as a good gift to be nurtured, protected, and restrained until its incredible power can be properly unleashed in marriage, we have used it as a means to make ourselves feel good or significant, or to escape the pain of our brokenness in other areas. For others, spiritual adultery has taken different forms: we have sat in the shade of money and power and said to our possessions, "You are my god." Or we have delighted in the sweet taste of the success that hard work and natural gifting bring us, saying to each accomplishment, "Wow! You are beautiful!" Such is our perversity that we can even make God's good gift of marriage and family into an idol, saying to ourselves, "If I don't have a good marriage or a successful family, then I am worthless." What is God to do with adulterous rebels like us?

The Lord does the same thing with us that Hosea did with Gomer, and that he did with Old Testament Israel. He pursues us out into the wilderness of our own making, where we end up cold, naked, isolated, and alone, drowning in shame, abandoned by the very things in which we put our trust. There, he calls us to come back to him. He wants you to know that even while your heart has been cold and hard toward him, his heart has remained dizzyingly, dazzlingly set on you. While you have been saying, "Wow! You are beautiful!" to all kinds of ugly substitutes, he still looks at you and says, "Wow! You are beautiful. You are a lily among the thorns. You are one of a kind, and *I still love you*." Even while you are running away, his loving heart still pursues you wherever you go.

The Proof of Love

Can this really be true? Is it possible to believe that such a crazy love really exists in a world of thorns and thistles, where so many people make grandiose promises to love you and then let you down? How can I know that such a love exists and that it includes me? God may feel that way about some people, like those who never miss their daily quiet time and perpetually ooze spirituality, but can he really love someone like me?

The proof of God's crazy love comes as we gaze at love's ultimate sacrifice on the cross. The cross flows from no ordinary love. Ordinary love loves those who love back. That is so often how we love, even within marriage. We love those who love us in return. If you have a good week of loving me, then you may expect to have a good week of my loving you. It is therefore natural for us to think that God loves us in that way: if I have a good week of doing what God tells me to do, then maybe he will love me. But God's dazzling, crazy love goes to those who did not love him. Even more, it goes to those who hated him, and cursed and crucified him—*to people just like us*. Jesus stretches out his wounded hands to us on the cross and says, "This is how much I love you." The Bible says, "God shows his love for us in that while we were still sinners, Christ died for us" (Rom. 5:8). Having shown us such love while we were still rebels against him, how will he not continue to love us with that same crazy, passionate delight now that we are his children? He says, "How can I give you up? I long to share a deep and intimate relationship with you forever. I will protect you and provide for you: come to my house of wine. Come sit under my banner, which is love."

The more we meditate on this crazy, dazzling, forgiving love for us, the more our love will be stirred toward him. Many Christians functionally view a relationship with God in the way traditional cultures view arranged marriages. We acknowledge that we need the Lord: someone has to protect and provide for us in this world. So we do the necessary chores that go with that relationship. We read our Bibles. We obey, more or less, the Christian rules. We go to church. But we are not dizzyingly, dazzlingly captivated by the Lord. We are not rearranging our lives daily so that we can arrange a "chance" meeting with him. We are not writing him love notes and embarrassing our friends because we constantly gush about the beauty of our Beloved. We are not waiting and longing for the day of his appearing. We have lost our first love for Christ. What is wrong with us?

The answer is that we have lost sight of his great love for us. We have taken our eyes off just how much we have been forgiven. In the midst of the busyness and pressures of life—studying and writing papers, meetings and memos, laundry and child care—we have missed Jesus. Yet each week as we come to church, the Lord invites us again into his house of wine. He does so not so that he can launch into his litany of all the ways in which we have failed him this week, but so that he can unfurl the banner of his love over us again and say to us, "Wow! You are beautiful! You are unique, one of a kind! I love you." As we come to worship, we are invited to see again just how beautiful a Savior Jesus is, just how brightly he shines.

It is no surprise that we fail to love Jesus as we ought. It is no surprise that we fail to love one another as we ought. The surprise is that he nonetheless loves us in a totally unexpected, undeserved, and overwhelming way that washes away all our sin and shame, and that will never let us go throughout eternity. Here is the truly crazy love that marriage and sex are designed to make us long for: God's amazing love for us in Jesus Christ.

4

Waiting

Song of Songs 2:8–17

Woman

8 The sound of my beloved!
Look, now he comes,
leaping over the mountains,
bounding over the hills.
9 My beloved is like a gazelle or a young stag.
Look, there he stands behind our wall,
gazing through the windows,
looking through the lattice.
10 My beloved speaks and says to me,

Man

"Arise, my darling, my beautiful one, and come away,
11 for look, the winter rains are past;
the spring rains have come and gone.
12 The blossoms appear on the earth,
the time of singing has come,
and the sound of the dove is heard in our land.
13 The fig tree ripens its figs,
and the vines are in blossom, emitting fragrance.
Arise, my darling, my beautiful one, and come away.

14 O my dove, in the clefts of the rock, in the crannies of the cliff,
let me see your form, let me hear your voice,
for your voice is sweet,
and your form is lovely."

Woman
15 "Catch the foxes for us,
the little foxes that spoil the vineyards,
for our vineyards are in blossom.
16 My beloved is mine, and I am his
—he who grazes among the lilies.
17 Until the day comes to life
and the shadows flee,
turn around, my beloved,
like a gazelle or a young stag on the mountains of Bether."

One of the agonizing aspects of being in love but not yet married is the need to wait. Sometimes the couple may live in two different towns or even two different countries. At other times, although you may live in the same town, there is the simple frustration of having to separate every night. You long for the day when your lives will be so intertwined that every aspect will be linked together. Part of that frustration, of course, is sex—or rather the longing for it. When my wife and I counsel engaged couples, they are sometimes embarrassed by how hard they find it to set proper boundaries on their physical intimacy. Yet even while there are very good reasons to wait faithfully for the honeymoon, as this passage emphasizes, it *should* be hard to wait. Don't be ashamed of this struggle. Be grateful as you wrestle with those desires and strive to remain pure.

On the other hand, if it is not difficult to wait for marriage in a serious relationship, that could be a sign that important issues need to be discussed. Perhaps you have been sexually abused, and your lack of desire is not godliness, but fear. Perhaps you grew up in a home environment that communicated loudly that sex is dirty or that good girls shouldn't enjoy it. Maybe you struggle with same-sex attraction, and though you are seeking to submit to God's design in marriage, desiring physical intimacy with the opposite sex is something that you will need to cultivate and pray for the Holy Spirit to give. Help is available in all these situations, but a lack of sexual desire could be a significant indicator that there are issues that need to be talked about, and perhaps counseling needed.

Part of the problem with waiting for sex for most of us is that in our culture we have lost the concept of waiting for anything. How many people still remember the days when you had to wait for the television to warm up after you turned it on before you could watch a program? Now we are used to instantly downloadable entertainment, readily available fast food, and the immediate gratification of all our desires. We don't save up to buy something that we want anymore. We just put it on our credit cards so that we can have it right away, and we get angry if anything prevents our immediate enjoyment of our desires. We don't want to wait for anything. Period. Yet this particular poem is all about waiting, even when the time seems absolutely, positively ripe. Some things are worth waiting for.

Come Away, My Love

The passage opens with the striking image of the man as the woman sees him, faster than a speeding bullet, stronger than a locomotive, leaping over not only tall buildings but entire mountains in his eagerness to get to her (Song 2:8). We can almost pick out the large *S* emblazoned on the chest of her Superman as he bounds like a gazelle or a young stag. But then the man comes screeching to a halt. He remains outside the wall of her house, desperately peering in at the window, through the lattice, trying somehow to make contact with her across this final boundary (v. 9). The couple's eyes meet, and the man launches into a wonderfully romantic speech so hauntingly beautiful that we want to cross-stitch it and hang it on the wall:

> Arise, my darling, my beautiful one, and come away,
> for look, the winter rains are past;
> the spring rains have come and gone.
> The blossoms appear on the earth,
> the time of singing has come,
> and the sound of the dove is heard in our land. (Song 2:10–12)

Apart from making most men feel inadequate because we have never uttered anything so romantic in our whole lives, what is going on here? Once we strip away the flowery poetry, what the man wants the woman to do is clear because he says it twice: "Arise, my darling, my beautiful one, and come away" (Song 2:10, 13). He wants her to leave the home of her father and mother, cross the wall, and join him on the other side, out where the deer and the antelope play.

What is more, the man gives a specific reason for her to make that move. The time is ripe, he says. This poem is tied to the end of the previous poem by the deer motif. At the end of the previous passage, the woman charged the daughters of Jerusalem by the gazelles and the does of the field not to stir up love before it pleases. Against the background of that vow by the gazelles not to stir up love until love itself is ready, here we see a gazelle bounding up to her to declare that the time for love has finally come.

How does the man know that the time for love is here? It is springtime. The winter rainy season has come and gone; the seasonal spring rains have also come and gone. Everything is bursting into bloom (Song 2:11–12)! The marks of spring's arrival are multisensory, pressing in on all sides: there is the sight of the blossoming flowers, the sound of the singing turtledoves, the fragrance of the blooms on the vines, and the taste of the ripening figs.[1] Every sensation cries out the message of nature that the time is right to find a partner and go forth, be fruitful, and multiply.

Why, then, should the woman continue to be like a dove in the clefts of the rock (Song 2:14)? Doves are timid creatures because they do not have much in the way of defense mechanisms: they don't have claws or teeth, or even particularly speedy flight. For safety, they have to rely on hiding in inaccessible locations where, even if you can see them, it is hard to get to them. So, too, from the man's perspective, the woman is like a dove: she is inaccessible to him on the other side of the wall, barred away on the far side of the lattice. She is tantalizingly visible, but out of reach. He can see her form and hear her voice, both of which are lovely. Yet he wants more. He longs for uninterrupted sound and sight, true and complete union.

Not Yet, My Love

But the woman says no. It is not that she isn't attracted to the man—far from it. That much has been clear from the opening verses of chapter 1,

1. *ʿēt hazzāmîr* could be translated as "the time of singing" (ESV) or "the time . . . for pruning" (NASB). Probably it is a pun that includes both meanings: *pruning* looks back to the previous image of blossoms, while *singing* looks forward to the next image of birdsong.

where she declared that his caresses were better than wine and that she could not wait for him to sweep her off her feet and carry her off to his chambers. Nor does the woman disagree with his declaration that it is springtime. On the contrary, she, too, says, "Our vineyards are in blossom" (Song 2:15). Remember that she has already used the image of the vineyard for her body, so she clearly understands what he is getting at. She is agreeing with him that both of them are physically mature enough for a relationship.

Yet the woman develops the young man's springtime metaphor in a different direction by reminding him of the danger that foxes posed to blooming vineyards during this season (Song 2:15). Remember, she says, that the tender new growth of blossoming vineyards is fragile and can easily be damaged. She does not unpack what specific dangers the foxes represent, perhaps because the danger is obvious enough. It is the danger posed by her going outside the wall to him at that time. It is not a harsh refusal, though. She does not say, "I can't believe you were thinking about *that*." In fact, there is a slightly teasing tone throughout her reply. She doesn't describe the danger as a big, bad wolf but rather as "little foxes," more of a nuisance than a fearsome threat. Yet her message is clear: even little foxes can damage the vineyard blossoms, and if they do so, the long-term effect on the fruit of the vineyard could be serious.

It is intriguing, too, that the appeal to "catch the foxes" has a plural subject ("y'all catch the foxes," as those from the American South might put it). This could simply be a rhetorical plural, a wish that is addressed to no one in particular.[2] Given the community that hovers in the background throughout the Song, however, it may be an implicit appeal to others to help the couple maintain the safety of their vineyards until the time is fully ripe for them to cross the wall and come together. It is a recognition that purity is not merely an individual decision but a community project. In the same way, when the wall that keeps him out was first mentioned, she called it "our wall." It seems clear that the *our* here is not the woman and the man: he is eager for the wall to disappear. Rather, the *our* is the woman and her family. The wall that protects her (and him) is a family matter, not just a personal commitment.

In spite of the woman's refusal to cross the wall to be with him at this time, she doesn't reject him or denigrate his desires. She still declares that

2. Michael V. Fox, *The Song of Songs and the Ancient Egyptian Love Songs* (Madison, WI: University of Wisconsin Press, 1985), 114.

her lover is hers and she is his, depicting him once again as a gazelle grazing among the lilies (Song 2:16). As so often in the Song, the exact referent of the image is elusive. Are the lilies on which she imagines him grazing her lips, as in 5:13, or another part of her anatomy, as in 7:2? At the very least, we can say that she still desires him physically, intensely. She, too, longs for the day when the wall will come down and all barriers between them are gone, so that she can fully be his and he can fully be hers forever.

Yet in spite of that ongoing, aching desire, she acknowledges that the time is not yet right. Until the day comes to life and the shadows flee away—that is, until the morning has fully come[3]—he will have to leave alone. For now, her young stag will have to go back to the mountains from whence he came, which she calls "the mountains of Bether." There is probably a double meaning in that name. On the one hand, "the mountains of Bether" is a known location west of Jerusalem, but more literally, the name means "the cleft mountains." You don't have to be Sigmund Freud to see a potential connection here to her breasts, a connection that will be made explicit later on in the Song. So even while she sends her man away for the time being, the very range of mountains upon which this gazelle is going to roam will constantly remind both of them of the destination to which they are ultimately headed and for which they are both longing. Her "No" is a "Not quite yet, my love," rather than a "Never."

The Wisdom of Delaying Sex until Marriage

What does this poem have to say to us in our own relationships? First, it clearly affirms the necessity and wisdom of delaying sexual activity. It was C. S. Lewis who said of biblical critics that they claim a remarkable ability to identify fern seeds while being unable to spot an elephant ten yards away in broad daylight.[4] So, too, it is striking how many scholars believe that the Song of Songs is a celebration of love and sex as being good in their own right without any reference to the social conventions of marriage. This is remarkable not simply because it requires taking the man's later references

3. The Hebrew of verse 17 literally says "until the day breathes," which could describe either the morning, when the day "comes to life," or the evening, when the cool breezes blow. But since this description is further qualified as the time when "the shadows flee," it fits better as a description of morning than of evening. See Fox, *Song of Songs and the Ancient Egyptian Love Songs*, 115.

4. C. S. Lewis, *Christian Reflections* (Grand Rapids: Eerdmans, 1994), 157.

to the woman as his "bride" in chapter 4 as purely metaphorical, which would be unique in both ancient and modern literature, but also because it misses what is as obvious as an elephant in broad daylight: that for all their eagerness to reach the consummation of their relationship, there are significant obstacles along the road. It is possible to stir up love too soon. There are little foxes that could harm their budding romance. Sometimes true love has to wait. What are they waiting for? Marriage, of course!

This message, as we have said, is countercultural in our context, which hates waiting for anything. The message that we receive, not just from those dreadfully dull and embarrassing high school sex-education classes but far more powerfully from contemporary movies, television sitcoms, and songs, is that we should wait only long enough to be physically ready for sex. Our culture asks, "Can you possibly be the only twenty-year-old in America who hasn't had at least one sexual relationship?" Of course, the actual statistics of abstinence are quite different, but that is not the message with which young people are bombarded. Meanwhile, the only dangerous "little fox" that our culture recognizes is sexually transmitted disease. So as long as you use a condom and practice "safe sex," there is nothing to worry about.

Meanwhile, conventional Christian wisdom tends to put a lot of stress on proper boundaries. We build dating parlors and come up with courtship plans and body maps of appropriate touch areas ("If it is covered by a bathing suit, then it is off-limits," as one presentation puts it, which makes some increasingly outdated assumptions about how extensive contemporary bathing suits are!). Thirty years ago, the mission that my wife Barb and I served with when we met in Africa had a rule that as an engaged couple we could never be alone together in a house without a chaperone. This simply encouraged us to be creative in bending the rules. I remember talking to another missionary from an earlier generation, who told me that in his day if an engaged couple went out on a walk at night together, they were required to take a light. "They didn't say that it had to be lit, though," he remarked, with a twinkle in his eye.

To this conventional wisdom, the Song of Songs replies with biblical wisdom. It shows us that the problem with conventional wisdom is not that it is necessarily wrong; rather, it is just too shallow. So when conventional societal wisdom warns us about sexually transmitted diseases, it is right to do so. Yet it neglects the fact that you can pick up heart wounds from sexual activity that will never show up on a test at a clinic. Other foxes can destroy the blossoms of your vineyard. Likewise, when conventional Christian wisdom focuses on boundaries, there is a measure of insight there. Proper boundaries are like the wall and the lattice in the passage. They can be helpful in delineating where the appropriate line is. But it is not the wall that keeps the woman inside. Walls have doors. They can be climbed over or tunneled under. Lattices can be forced open. The only thing that will keep her and him on separate sides of that wall until marriage is a heart commitment that flows out of a grasp of true wisdom.

Rules and Reasons

This desire for rules is true much more broadly in our lives than merely in our sexuality. In many areas of life, we demand guidance, often with much more specificity than anything found in God's Word. How many minutes a day should I read my Bible and pray? What percentage of my income should I give to the church? How far is too far when we are dating? Yet the problem with rules is that they easily lead to pride or guilt. If I keep my (man-made) rule, then I feel proud and look down on others who don't achieve the same standards that I do. If I fail and break the rule, then either I reinterpret the rule to match my performance or I feel crushingly guilty over my failure. This is particularly true when it comes to Christian rules for sexuality. We become masters at justifying why a particular behavior doesn't count as sex, or we ache with intense guilt over our repeated failure.

What this poem in the Song of Songs gives us, however, is not a rule but a reason. In the face of springtime hormones that are crying out with every fiber of our being that now is the time to be fruitful and multiply, the Song reminds us that those pesky little foxes cause very real damage and get in the way of the ultimate goal of the vineyard, which is bearing rich fruit. The farmer who invests energy in protecting the integrity of the vineyard will not regret it later, even though he or she won't reap the benefits of this painful perseverance until the time is fully ripe.

It is unfortunate, therefore, that the focus of Christian sex education is usually on abstinence. Abstinence, by definition, focuses attention on what you are *not* doing. Abstain from anything, and the chances are that you will feel deprived. Tell teenagers to abstain from something, and you are almost inviting them to explore it. Likewise, the Christian fascination with "purity rings" is a rule-based approach that tends to make protecting one's vineyard sound like a one-shot deal. The intention to commit to a lifetime of purity may be wonderful, but think about the devastating implications of this very visible commitment. If you fail sexually, even once, then you have to either turn in your ring or get really good about lying. How many people do you know who are willing at such a vulnerable stage of their lives to face the ignominy of taking off their rings, thereby making a public declaration to their family and friends of what just happened? So now we add lying to sexual sin, and we become experts at justifying why what we did doesn't really count as sex and why we are still virgins in our hearts.

Vineyard Tending

By contrast, biblical wisdom speaks of purity as watching over the blossoms in a vineyard. Vineyard tending is a long, patient process of waiting and watching in which one failure does not bring the whole endeavor to nothing. The farmer who fails does not have to give up the vineyard as damaged goods. He or she can repent and rebuild the broken wall and start again to watch and to wait. Equally, while keeping the walls is important in vineyard tending, it is not the only thing. It is really about taking care of the tender blossoms. This means that tending your sexual vineyard is not just about refraining from actual physical sexual intercourse; it is about protecting your mind from habitual lust, romantic fantasy, and pornography, all of which can have short- and long-term damaging effects. You can have a vineyard whose walls are still intact—technically, you are still a virgin and can wear the ring—but whose blossoms have been trampled into the muddy dirt in many other ways.

This watching and waiting over the vineyard is not an end in itself. Rather, it has a wonderful purpose. At the end of the process, you want to present your vineyard to your lover in full bloom, so that you can both graze among the lilies without regret or remorse. The intensity of the waiting makes the final consummation all the more glorious. Instead of leading to guilt or pride, sexual failure should lead us to repentance and restoration, while God-enabled purity should bring profound thankfulness for God's grace that has protected us against ourselves.

So how do we help one another to protect the tender blossoms in the vineyards? How do we rebuild and restore vineyards that are broken down? To begin with, as couples enter relationships, we need to focus on reasons, not just rules. Rules can be helpful to set boundaries, but only if you already know the reasons why you have set those rules. Otherwise, one or both of you are going to keep chipping away at the rules until you find yourselves much further along the road to physical intimacy than you expected. But if you both know and remind yourselves regularly why you are waiting—so that you can joyfully present your vineyard to your spouse within marriage without damage or regret—then it will help you to keep the boundaries in the proper places.

Do not expect yourselves as a newly minted couple to have the wisdom that you need. The wise farmer does not rely on catching all the little foxes himself. He calls in his friendly neighborhood pest exterminator. So, too, we were not made to live as individuals, or as couples, but in community, where we share wisdom together. We need others to shed light into our blindness, to help us make good decisions. If you are entering a relationship, get advice from wise older people about what good boundaries are. Have people praying for you specifically. For some, that godly wisdom can come from parents. Others will have to search out other godly older people to guide and help them.

In addition, make provision for your weakness. Expect yourselves to be very weak, and so don't put yourselves in situations in which the temptation will be overwhelming. For example, I have had couples tell me that after graduation they plan to live in an apartment together but not have sex. That is like inviting the foxes over to camp out in your vineyard but hoping that they won't touch the blossoms. We are weak people who are easily led astray, and our sexual drives are very powerful. So be wise about the plans that you make about when and how you are alone together.

Hope Deferred

So far, I have talked about watching over your vineyard and preparing for the fruitful harvest as if that final outcome were guaranteed. I have made it sound as though every good farmer who tends his or her vineyard carefully will ultimately enjoy the fruit of those long, hard labors. What about those who are long-term single, however, or those who struggle with same-sex attraction? The same sexual desires may be there, yet there is no plausible end to your waiting in sight. You don't see any way in which these blossoming vines that you are tending will ever bear fruit in a biblically approved sexual relationship. So why should you continue to take good care of your vineyard? You know exactly what the writer of Proverbs means when he says, "Hope deferred makes the heart sick" (Prov. 13:12). To you, "Not yet" seems like "Never." Meanwhile, your springtime is turning to summer, then autumn: the flowers fade, the blossoms drop from your vines, and there is no fruitful harvest. Under those circumstances, watching and waiting can easily seem like so much wasted labor.

There are at least two reasons for us still to wait and watch. The first and less important reason is that God may surprise us with an unexpected relationship. A person who has been single for many years may finally meet a godly spouse. Men and women whose struggle is with same-sex attraction, or with other kinds of sexual brokenness, do in many cases get successfully married to a person of the opposite gender. There is, after all, a lot more to a great marriage than sex! Do not discount God's remarkable ability to confound your "doom and gloom" predictions for the future. He is the God who does far more than all that we can ask or imagine (Eph. 3:20).

The second, and far more important, reason is that whether or not we ever get married and find a beautiful and legitimate outlet for God-given sexual desires, there is a greater Lover for whom we are waiting. No mere human being can really leap over the mountains and bound over the hills. It is poetic hyperbole. Yet if you are a Christian, you have a Lover who truly loves you like that. There is a God who desires you so passionately that he has moved heaven and earth to have a relationship with you. There is a heavenly Bridegroom who doesn't just gaze at us longingly from a distance but bursts through the walls that we have erected to keep him out so that he can sweep us off our feet. The powerful sexual drives that God has given to cement us together in marriage are but a pale reflection of just how passionately and intensely God desires to be bonded to us.

In Isaiah 5:1–7, the prophet sings a song of his Beloved who had a vineyard. This Beloved took perfect care of his vineyard: he dug it, cleared it of stones, and fertilized it; he built a wall around it and put a watchtower in the middle to keep guard against the foxes and other intruders. Yet when it came harvest time, the Beloved found only a few sour and bitter grapes on the vines.

Isaiah was describing God's love relationship with his people, Israel, but he could just as easily have been describing the Lord's relationship with you and me. The Lord has given us so much. He has taken such good care of us and given us abundant gifts—beauty, intellect, wealth, talent, opportunity, relationships, life itself—but what fruit have we borne for him? Wild and sour grapes. Specifically in the area of our sexuality, he has given each of us a beautiful vineyard to watch over, and we have razed the wall, invited the foxes in for a party, planted thorns and thistles, and turned the whole thing into a muddy and sordid mess. Some of us have ruined our vineyards through sex outside marriage, others through lust, pornography, or illicit fantasies. Still others of us are perhaps proud that we have preserved the sanctity of our vineyards, but we haven't really protected them; we have despised them. Hating sex and closing down the vineyard completely can be just another way of destroying a good gift that God has given us. A typical landowner would call the police in to arrest his tenants if they behaved like that.

But God is not any normal landowner. Instead, he sent his own Son to rescue and redeem his tenants from their own folly. Jesus came from the vast glory and perfection of heaven and entered the muddy mess of this world in order to rebuild his vineyard (see John 15). He came as a normal man, with normal sexual desires that he knew he would not be able to fulfill. Yet Jesus guarded his vineyard perfectly, watching over it and waiting, not for the sake of a future earthly bride but for the sake of his heavenly bride, the church. The bride that he chose for himself has no beauty of her own, for she has not kept her own vineyard. She is grimy and dressed in the filthy rags of her abused sexuality. Yet her Beloved came to clothe her in the beautiful garments of his own faithful watching and waiting, so that on her wedding day, she could be presented pure and spotless, without blemish, beautiful beyond description (Rev. 19:7–8; see Eph. 5:26–27). This is the Lover for whom we are all watching and waiting, whether single or married, hopeful or hopeless, straight or struggling with same-sex attraction. This is the Lover who now calls us to maintain our vineyards as best we can and has promised to aid us in our struggle.

Hope Fulfilled

Hope deferred makes the heart sick. Some of us know all too well what this feels like. Some of us are sick of watching and waiting, and have given in to many temptations. The fantasies of our hearts and minds reveal the fact that while we say that we are waiting for Jesus, in reality our longing is simply to find a man or a woman who will make us feel good. We have sick hearts as well as sullied vineyards. Can there really be hope for people like us?

Yet the proverb goes on: "but a desire fulfilled is a tree of life" (Prov. 13:12). We are not just to watch and wait and guard our vineyards for the sake of an earthly harvest, a wonderful vintage marriage to a good Christian man or woman. That is a beautiful desire if it is God's plan for you (and God's grace is often so much greater than we deserve). He can restore the broken-down vineyard and replant the blossoms that the foxes have eaten. In his kindness, God often treats us far better than we deserve. In his grace, he will even use our sexual sin to grow us and glorify himself.

But it is not just for this life that we are to guard our vineyards against the foxes. There is an ultimate harvest, a tree of life whose fruit we will taste on the last day, when Jesus' waiting and ours finally comes to an end with the return of the Bridegroom to claim his bride. On that day, he will finally come leaping over the mountains and bounding over the hills to claim his people. On that day, there will be no more wall to separate us, no more looking and longing from a distance. On that day, our cold and wandering hearts will finally be transformed and made whole. We will behold the loveliness of his form with our own eyes. On that day, it will be springtime and harvest all together, as Jesus says to us, his people:

> Arise, my darling, my beautiful one, and come away,
> for look, the winter rains are past;
> the spring rains have come and gone.
> The blossoms appear on the earth,
> the time of singing has come,
> and the sound of the dove is heard in our land.
> The fig tree ripens its figs,
> and the vines are in blossom, emitting fragrance.
> Arise, my darling, my beautiful one, and come away. (Song 2:10–13)

Have you heard and responded to his invitation? Can you say today of Jesus, "My beloved is mine and I am his, forever and forever"? Today, he calls you to come and lay down your heart before him. Don't let your sin and brokenness keep you away—he died to pay for each of those sins. Don't let your own attempts at goodness keep you away—you could never be good enough to match up to God's perfect standard. Come to the Beloved who calls to you, "Arise, my darling, my beautiful one, and come away."

In the meantime, as we battle hearts that wander far more than they wait, we have been given the Word and the sacraments to help us as a community. We gather around the Bible week after week and are reminded that God loves us with such intensity that he was willing to watch his beloved only Son be tortured to death for us. As we break the bread and share the cup, we rehearse the truth again: his body was broken for us; his blood was shed for our redemption. His arms were stretched open wide to receive the sexually broken: Hosea's wife, Gomer (Hos. 1–3); the woman of Samaria, who had been through five husbands and was living with yet another partner (John 4); the prostitute who washed Jesus' feet with her tears (Luke 7:37–48); the woman taken in the very act of adultery (John 8:3–11); the list goes on and on to include you and me. Broken people, with devastated vineyards, are welcomed by his grace into a new family of forgiveness, hope, and life. Broken people, who know that they have no righteousness of their own to offer, find hope in the righteousness that Jesus Christ himself provides.

We wait. But waiting is not forever. So wait with patience for that great day, when your hopes will finally be fulfilled. Look forward to your wedding feast that is yet to come, when all of life's disappointments and failures will be past, and we will joyfully drink the wedding cup of the new covenant in heaven, with Jesus.

5

SEARCHING

Song of Songs 3:1–5

Woman
3:1 Upon my bed night after night
I sought the one whom my soul loves.
I sought him but did not find him.
2 Therefore, I will arise and go around the city;
in the streets and plazas I will seek the one whom my soul loves.
I sought him but I did not find him.
3 The guards who go around the city found me:
"The one whom my soul loves—have you seen [him]?"
4 Only a little [while] after I passed on from them,
I found the one whom my soul loves.
I seized him and would not leave him alone
until I could bring him to the house of my mother,
to the chamber where she conceived me.
5 I charge you, daughters of Jerusalem,
by the gazelles or the does of the field,
that you will not arouse or awaken love
until it delights.

What is so great about love? According to brand-new lovers, everything. It is a dizzying, dazzling emotion that lifts you up to the heavens. You feel amazing, ecstatic. With Eliza Doolittle in *My Fair Lady*, you feel that you could dance all night—and then go on some more. But then the night sets in, and you are all alone, and you start to wonder. Is this real? Does he actually love me? Will it truly last? Is this forever? You find yourself saying like Shakespeare's Juliet, "It is too rash, too unadvised, too sudden; too like the lightning, which doth cease to be ere one can say 'It lightens.'"[1] As this passage in the Song of Songs reminds us, as well as being dizzying and dazzling, love is often painful, frustrating, and confusing, as we search for a deep intimacy that keeps escaping us. That is true both in our human relationships and in our search for God. In this chapter, therefore, as we examine the frustrating side of the search for intimacy, we will think about why we should keep on searching for love in the midst of its challenges, as well as of the ultimate joyful conclusion to that search.

A Dream of Searching

This poem presents us with a recurrent dream of searching, with which the woman wrestles night after night.[2] In the previous poem, she was confident and assured in sending the man away until morning came. She knew that it was not yet time for them to be together permanently. Now, though, as the long nights alone stretch on, she seems less sure of that decision, and in her dreams she ventures outside the wall of her house, searching for her beloved. Of course, many of our dreams revolve around looking for something. It may be something ridiculous—seeking an elephant in a department store, perhaps—or something profound. Dreams are often puzzling and confusing, combining scenes in which the familiar and the bizarre merge and melt, but they are frequently connected to our deepest desires. In the woman's dream, she is constantly searching for her man, whom she repeatedly calls "the one whom my soul loves" (Song 3:1, 2, 3, 4; cf. 1:7).

Her first attempt to find the man while she remained at home failed: "I sought him but did not find him" (Song 3:1). In the dream, her next search took her out into the streets and open areas of the city, which would have been dangerous territory for a young girl to venture into alone at night, then as now. Yet this second attempt also ended in failure: "I sought him but I did

1. *Romeo and Juliet*, act 2, scene 2.

2. The Hebrew word *balleylot* could simply mean "by night" (ESV), but the plural form seems to suggest that this is a repeated exercise. Compare the other occurrences of the form in Psalms 92:3[2]; 134:1; and Song 3:8.

not find him" (v. 2). Immediately after this second failure, she herself was found by the watchmen who go around the city. There is a certain irony in this: the seeker was found by those who weren't looking for her. Surely if anyone would have known where her beloved was, it would be these men, whose job it was to observe everyone and everything that went on in the city. So she asked them: "The one whom my soul loves—have you seen him?" (v. 3). But they had not seen him either. Three attempts to find the one whom her soul loves, and three failures.

But then, at last, success! Just a little while after she left the watchmen, she finally found the one whom her soul loves (Song 3:4). In her dream, she seized him and refused to let him go until she had safely brought him to her mother's house, to the very room where she herself was conceived. And at that point, the author wisely drops the curtain on the dream. We don't need to hear what happens next. We can imagine the rest—a satisfactory conclusion to her imaginings. Instead, he concludes with a repetition of the cautionary refrain that we met in the previous chapter: "Daughters of Jerusalem, . . . [do] not arouse or awaken love until it delights" (v. 5). Love is not all wine and roses, moonlight in Paris and soaring emotional highs: it can sometimes be a pit of uncertainty and darkness, in which you wander around, afraid that you have lost the one your soul loves. You fear ending up by yourself in a lonely room, listening to sad songs on the radio, surrounded by used tissues, lamenting your loss. The cautionary note of the Song of Songs is strong in this chapter, even though on this occasion the dream has a happy ending, and it behooves us to heed its warning well.

The Pursuit of Intimacy

So what does this cautionary dream have to teach us? The first and fairly obvious lesson is that love is hard work. True intimacy must be persistently pursued in discomforting and (emotionally, at least) dangerous ways. Love is not a state into which you effortlessly fall but a relationship in which you repeatedly search for your beloved until you find him or her. As the old saying goes, "If at first you don't succeed, try, try again." When the woman finally found her man, she seized him and would not let him go. *Seize* is the same word that she used in the previous section about catching the foxes

(Song 2:15). There is a tenacity and a focus to her pursuit of the man here; this is not merely casual dating in which two members of the opposite sex are hanging out in a long-term undefined relationship. Love involves an exclusive pursuit—he is "the one whom my soul loves," not "one of many possible romantic candidates." What is more, it is a pursuit with a clear goal, which is to "bring him to the house of my mother, to the chamber where she conceived me" (3:4).

Why does the woman want to bring the man to her mother's house, of all places? Well, she clearly has sexual fulfillment in mind, as most commentators have observed.[3] That is no surprise, given what we have already seen in the Song of Songs, and what we already know about teenagers in love. As we have said earlier, the eager desire for sex is not denigrated or squelched but affirmed as something good and appropriate, not just for young men but for young women as well—which would have been countercultural in its ancient context.

Yet we should also recognize that in her dreams this young woman doesn't simply long for sex: she longs for sex in the appropriate context—the context of home and family. If all she wanted was sex, she could have gone outside the wall with him in the previous poem. It is much easier to get privacy out in the fields than it is within the family home. Yet in her dream, when she finds him she doesn't take him out into the woods. She wants to bring him to the house of her mother, to the very chamber where she was conceived. What she means by that is that she wants to bring the man into the epicenter of her life and her own family history, so that he can understand on a deep level what profound influences have shaped her into the person that she is.

In other words, what the woman dreams of and longs for is a deep intimacy with the one whom her soul loves, a relationship in which their souls are entwined together as intimately as their bodies. She wants to bring him to the place where together they can form the next generation of the family, just as when, after Sarah's death, Isaac took his wife Rebekah into Sarah's tent and was comforted (Gen. 24:67). To use the language of Genesis 2:24, she wants the man to leave his father and his mother and be joined to his wife and the two become one flesh, with all that that entails for the complete meshing of their lives.

3. See Richard S. Hess, *Song of Songs*, BCOTWP (Grand Rapids: Baker Academic, 2005), 106.

That image of a deeply committed relationship is countercultural in our context. We often view the dating process as a rather casual and individual process in which we "try on" various relationships in order to find the person who makes us feel good. Alternatively, we maintain a relationship simply because having someone—anyone—in our life feels better than being alone. In the wider culture, that approach leads to a pattern of serial relationships and casual hookups, in which people become "friends with benefits," because sex feels good but we can't imagine making an exclusive commitment to one person, at least not yet. There are all kinds of reasons for that selfish individualism and fear of commitment, not least the breakdown in the marriages that we see all around us, and that in many cases we have experienced within our own families. So we disconnect sex from commitment, and commitment from relationships, which turns us into consumers of relationships. We are constantly searching for people we can use to serve our interests and meet our needs, rather than looking for a single, lifelong intimate relationship in which we become the committed servant of another with whom our life is utterly and eternally intertwined.

Against that contemporary view, the Song urges us to respect the awesome and disturbing power of love and sex. Do not treat sex as a light thing, something that can easily be toyed with. Don't play around with casual relationships. Until you are ready to commit to this kind of all-consuming search for the one whom you are going to incorporate into your family and with whom you will build the next generation, you are not ready for love, and you are certainly not ready for sex.

Sometimes we love the feeling of being in a relationship more than we actually love the other person. But the love of being in a relationship won't keep us going when the other person's sins and failings become clear, as they inevitably will sooner or later, because the other person is a sinner. But if our soul truly loves a person with a deep and unshakable love, whether the person is present or absent, then we will continue to pursue that one and seek his or her best even when the person's very worst is on display. When you are single, it is easy to focus on the challenge of getting into a relationship in the first place. However hard that process may be, though, entering into a relationship is the easy part; truly loving someone is very hard.

That explains why it makes sense to get to know someone really well before you commit to joining your lives together. To be sure, if you are going to get married, you will have to marry a sinner, because that is the only kind of person there is. Yet not every sinner is an equally good match for you. There are some people who encourage you to be a better person when you are with them. Meanwhile, there are others who don't have that impact on you, even though they may themselves be quite good people. The period of dating or courtship is not simply to be spent in a glorious romantic haze. It is supposed to be the time when you gather the data about how you fit together as a couple, how effectively you serve each other, and how effectively you serve others together.

Of course, the Bible also insists that you need to marry a Christian—someone who shares your deepest values and loves. Paul uses the vivid image of being "unequally yoked" (2 Cor. 6:14). Imagine a little donkey and a massive ox yoked to the same plow. How can they possibly hope to plow a straight furrow together? They are mismatched and will inevitably end up pulling in different directions, so the plow will go all over the place. So, too, how can you, as a Christian, possibly hope to plow a straight furrow with someone who doesn't share your most important values, hopes, and dreams? How can you become bone of my bone, flesh of my flesh, and soul of my soul with someone whose soul is not in tune with yours at the deepest level? God *may* change someone profoundly after your marriage, so that your spouse comes to share your faith or your level of commitment to Christianity. But that isn't usually what happens. God can miraculously turn donkeys into oxen, but that doesn't make yoking a donkey together with an ox and hoping for the best a wise farming strategy! Better to keep on searching for a more equal and God-honoring match, even though that search for love is long and arduous and suffers repeated failures along the way.

Continuing the Lifelong Search for Intimacy

Paradoxically, the quest doesn't end when the woman enters a relationship. In one sense, the woman in the poem has already found her man. She's not searching the streets for someone to love but rather trying to connect with the one person that she already loves. Having found her man, she keeps on looking for him. Relationships are never static; they are always going somewhere. You are either moving closer together or drifting farther apart. The woman is clear about where she wants this relationship to go: onward to marriage and to family. In pursuit of that goal, she undergoes considerable discomfort and risk in her dream, which is quite revealing. She can't find intimacy with her man by staying at home in her comfortable bed. If she wants to find him, she will have to go out and search the dark streets. Once she finds him, she will seize him and bring him home. These are active images. So how active are you in your relationships? Are they going somewhere? Are you having meaningful conversations that build intimacy, or are you simply killing time together? Are you exploring family backgrounds and discussing the shaping influences and experiences that make you who you are? Are you talking about goals and interests, the people that you hope to become? Does your faith constantly surface in those conversations as a central factor in defining who you are at the core of your being? Or do you just chat endlessly about trivia?

Nor does that need to keep searching for each other and going somewhere in your relationship end with a wedding, as we will see in the parallel dream in chapter 5. Many couples work very hard to get to know each other before they get married, and then assume that they can live on autopilot afterward. He is off doing his work, perhaps, while she is investing heavily in the children. Twenty-five years later, the children go off to college and the couple wake up to discover that they now know next to nothing about this person with whom they are living. Searching for the one your soul loves is to be a lifelong endeavor, a life-shaping passion, not a brief season.

The Cost of Intimacy

Sometimes intimate conversations are risky and even painful. It can be hard to open up to someone else about the deep wounds of the past and present struggles. It can be risky to trust someone with information that he or she could easily use to hurt you. This kind of emotional intimacy doesn't (and shouldn't) happen on a first date. But it is an essential part of building a deep and real relationship that bonds you together profoundly and prepares you for marriage. After all, how the person responds to this information is crucial to knowing how he or she will care for you and encourage you in the future hurts and struggles of life. It is an essential part of the search for the one your soul is called to love.

Some conversations may also need to involve other people, which cuts against our individualistic approach to building relationships. When the woman wants to bring her beloved to the house of her mother, it is reasonable to assume that she wants him to meet her! Our families often know us and love us better than anyone else and can help us to wisely evaluate the health of our relationships. Building a strong relationship is a community project, as we have seen. If you don't have a wise family to guide you in this area, find other mature mentors who can help you to discern whether your relationship is progressing in healthy ways. Think about seeking out pre-premarital counseling together as you take seriously the awesome weightiness of the commitment that you are thinking about making.[4]

At this point, some of you may think, "If finding a love relationship is this hard, maybe I had better stay single." What if you put in all that effort and take all that risk and end up being let down and abandoned? What if your searching does not end up with finding? Love is risky; to set your heart on one person inevitably means facing up to the fear of losing him or her.

Such a concern is not a bad response to this passage. This poem has a strong cautionary tone, as the conclusion shows: it may be perfectly appropriate for you to conclude that right now you are not yet ready for this kind of search. That is wise. Resist the cultural pressure suggesting that you have to be in a serious relationship right now or you are likely to be on the shelf forever. Not having an engagement ring by the spring of your college graduation year does not mean that you are bound for permanent spinsterhood or bachelorhood. In God's good providence, there is a time and a season for love that is unique to each relationship, and you don't have to rush into it. But when you do, make sure that you are ready to pursue love through to its proper conclusion with the due diligence and single-minded focus that it demands. Of course, true love doesn't always wait for a convenient time in your schedule. Its overwhelming power can break in upon you at any time, but you don't need

4. A helpful resource on this topic is David Powlison and John Yenchko, *Pre-Engagement: Five Questions to Ask Yourselves* (Phillipsburg, NJ: P&R Publishing, 2000).

to keep poking it with a stick, trying to make love happen, when the time is really not right.

Intimacy with God

So far, we have simply talked about our search for human relationships. Yet our search for love on the human level mirrors and mimics our search for the love of God. The woman's search for the man through the streets of the city echoes the competing voices of Dame Wisdom and Lady Folly in the book of Proverbs, crying out on the street corners to draw people to themselves (Prov. 9). Indeed, searching for a relationship with God is a key theme in the parables of Jesus. He declares that the kingdom of God is like a man who found a treasure buried in a field. He sold everything that he had in order to buy the field. The kingdom of God is like a pearl of great price; the man who found that pearl also sold everything he had in order to purchase it (Matt. 13:44–46). If developing a human relationship demands a passionate, single-minded, and risky pursuit, what should we say about our search for God? Are you pursuing intimacy with him with the same passion with which you pursue earthly relationships? Or are you involved in a casual, consumer relationship with God, in which you hang out with him as long as it seems to benefit you but shy away from a deeper and more costly commitment to know, love, and serve him as your true and eternal soulmate?

In exactly the same way that our culture often depicts falling in love as a one-time experience that just happens to you, so, too, there are people who think the same way about their relationship with God. Perhaps you made a commitment to Christ as a result of an experience at a camp or at a church event, but that is the extent of your relationship. Or maybe you regularly come to church on Sunday because that's what you were brought up to do, but during the rest of the week Jesus fades into the background. That is not the way the Bible describes a relationship with God. The psalmist says, "As a deer pants for flowing streams, so pants my soul for you, O God" (Ps. 42:1). The psalmist thirsted for God as an animal deprived of liquid sustenance in the wilderness longs for a flowing brook. Ponder this image. Does the deer casually search for water and get distracted if it doesn't immediately find some? No! Its whole being is bound up in the desperate search for something to drink: if it doesn't find that stream, it will die. Does a similar desperation characterize your search for God?

If you are anything like me, the answer is "I am afraid not." I don't have that desperation because frankly—and wrongly—most of the time I believe that I can get along just fine without God in my life. Because I feel functionally able to make good decisions for myself and believe that I have the strength to live my life reasonably well, I don't feel the crushing, desperate need to search for God. That is one reason, of course, why God in his grace and mercy sometimes chooses to expose the folly of my self-confidence (see Westminster Confession of Faith 5.5). He can do that in a variety of ways. He may do it through bringing me into overwhelming circumstances, in which sickness, pain, and bereavement leave me evidently unable to cope. He may do it by turning me over to my sinful desires, so that I sin in ways I had not thought possible before. He may do it by withdrawing the light of his presence for a while, in order that I may see how dark and empty my life truly is without the joy of his salvation.

All these things feel like a kind of death, but they are actually the Lord's loving invitation to search for life—to stop drinking water from the stale cisterns of our own making and to go looking for streams of living water (see Jer. 2:13). The reason that the dream was such a powerful experience for the woman was the intensity of the search—she didn't find the man right away and had to keep on searching for him. As a result, when she finally tracked him down and embraced him, her joy was all the greater. So, too, God may hide his presence from us and leave us in a dry and thirsty desert for a while, exposed to the reality of our own sin and the painful brokenness and emptiness of this world, not because he hates us but precisely because he loves us. He loves us far too much to let us be content with the shallow diversions and joy substitutes with which we so often content ourselves. So he takes them away, and we toss and turn on our beds night after night, finally starting to search for him.

The Hiddenness of God

For some, the painful loss and the hiddenness of God come precisely in the context of our love relationships. We experience broken friendships, shattered marriages, and crippled families that leave us wounded and lonely.

Sometimes we wonder what we did wrong that caused things to turn out this way. At other times, we are all too aware of what we did wrong, but are now unable to retrieve the situation. Some of us have never found the kind of intimate relationship for which we so deeply long. Our searching for love has come up empty. Sometimes there is a painful mismatch between our desire for love and the teaching of God's Word, as in the case of those who wrestle with same-sex attraction or feelings of love for someone who is not a believer. Every time we see others searching for and finding the one their soul loves, we feel the black night of our own loneliness pressing in upon us all the more intensely.

The black darkness of our night is actually God's invitation to us to search for him—to search diligently, eagerly, longingly, as the woman in the poem searches for her man and the deer searches for flowing streams. Yet the good news of the gospel is that the One for whom we search is not playing hide-and-seek with us. He, too, is searching for us. Alongside the parables of the kingdom that depict us as searching for the kingdom like treasure, Jesus also told a series of parables about God's search for sinners. In Luke 15, there is a shepherd who has a hundred sheep and loses just one; he goes out and searches for it and brings it safely home with rejoicing. There is a woman who has ten coins and loses one. Probably these were no ordinary coins but part of a special necklace or headband that she had worn at her wedding. To lose such a coin would be like losing a wedding ring, so she searches diligently until she finds it. Upon finding it, she throws a party for all her neighbors to celebrate. Finally, there is the climactic parable of the lost son, whose father waits for him eagerly, with aching longing for his return.

Thus our search for God is not an attempt to track down a distant, elusive deity who is capriciously hiding himself. Your heavenly Father is not a deadbeat dad who doesn't want to be bothered by his kids. The wonderful news about our search for God is that our Father is out every day, scanning the horizon for the first sign of our return so that he can run to us, scoop us up in his arms, and delight in our presence. You can't lose God. Even in the blackest night of your soul, when God feels most distant and far away, he is always there with his arms wide open, waiting for you to feel your emptiness and run to him, welcoming you to share intimacy with him at the banqueting table in his house.

Stirring Up Our Longing for God

How can we stir up our soul's love for God? Where can we find him when he seems distant from us? The answer to both of these questions is the same: we find him in his coming to us in Jesus Christ. The story of Zacchaeus makes this clear. Zacchaeus was living a broken life. He was a tax collector—not something that good little Jewish boys wanted to be when they grew up. It meant that he was collaborating with the hated Roman invaders, getting rich through imposing their oppressive fees on an impoverished people. Yet Zacchaeus was curious. Luke tells us that he was seeking to see who Jesus was. He climbed a sycamore tree to see this celebrity as he passed by, and he must have been astonished to hear Jesus call out to him, "Zacchaeus, hurry and come down, for I must stay at your house today" (Luke 19:5). That day, Zacchaeus found Jesus and also found a new direction for his life, in which he joyfully announced his repentance by repaying all those whom he had defrauded. But Jesus put Zacchaeus's searching and finding in context when he proclaimed, "Today salvation has come to this house, . . . for the Son of Man came to seek and to save the lost" (vv. 9–10). Zacchaeus found the One who had come to seek him.

Are you lost today? Come to the One who is searching for you. In Jesus Christ, God came to seek and to save you. It was a risky, costly venture for Jesus. For him, it was not just a disturbing dream. It was a journey away from the comfort and glory of heaven into the dark, broken wilderness of this world. He entered relationships in which he would be hurtfully disappointed and betrayed by those whom he most loved, as the disciples abandoned him and fled, denying that they even knew him. He came into a hungry and thirsty wilderness, where he faced Satan's fiercest temptations: "If you are the Son of God, command these stones to become loaves of bread" (Matt. 4:3). Yet he answered faithfully, "Man shall not live by bread alone, but by every word that comes from the mouth of God" (v. 4). He truly hungered and thirsted for God, not for the moldy rations provided by idols. Yet we took this searching Shepherd and nailed him to a cross, rejecting his glorious kingdom in pursuit of our own petty kingdoms. We did not want what he was offering; we were not searching for him. We were content to be lost.

Yet it wasn't just our rejection that hurt Jesus on the cross. The greatest pain that he endured on that day was gazing upward, searching for the answering smile of the Father, and finding nothing. The Father turned his face away from the Son as the tidal wave of our sin engulfed him. In order to seek and to save the lost, Jesus himself had to endure being lost. What cost he suffered for our sake!

Precisely in that moment of his greatest pain, however, as the Son of Man was lifted up on the cross, he was made most visible to all the longing eyes that God has opened. He became a beacon of hope for all those who are searching, for all those whom the Lord our God is calling to himself. Now he stands in heaven, raised up from the dead, victoriously calling all those whom the Father has given him. Behold your God, the One crucified to win you back and raised for your vindication, the One whom your soul was made to love, and the One who has loved you and cared for you so intensely! Here is the One for whom you have been searching your whole life. Come, bow down before him and receive him as your Lord; as you come to him, let the Father enfold you in his loving arms.

Then, when you find that your heart is cold toward God and inclined to give up on the search for him, meditate again on Jesus' costly search for you. Give thanks for his persistence and single-minded focus on seeking and saving those who are lost. He will not lose a single one of those who belong to him, and even your frustrating search for him is part of his perfect work within you. Give thanks that his faithful search for God while he lived here on earth is now credited to your account. Look forward to the day when our feverish dreams of searching and not finding will finally be over, as the King of kings welcomes us into his nearer presence. On that day, he will bring us to his own house and lift us into his arms, where we will be found forever.

6

Money Can't Buy Love

Song of Songs 3:6—4:7

Man
6 Who is this coming up from the wilderness
like columns of smoke,
perfumed with myrrh and frankincense
from all of the merchant's fragrant powders?

7 Behold! His bed—Solomon's—sixty mighty men surrounding it
from the mighty men of Israel!
8 All of them skilled swordsmen, experienced in battle,
each with his sword by his side
because of the terrors of the night.
9 King Solomon made a bed for himself
from the wood of Lebanon.
10 Its posts he made of silver,
its roof of gold, its seat of purple,
its interior inlaid with love
by the daughters of Jerusalem.
11 Go out and look at King Solomon, daughters of Zion,
wearing the crown with which his mother crowned him
on the day of his wedding,
on the day of his heart's rejoicing.

4:1 Behold, you are beautiful, my darling!
Behold, you are beautiful!
Your eyes are doves behind your veil.
Your hair is like a flock of goats
streaming down from Mount Gilead.
2 Your teeth are like a flock of newly sheared sheep
which are going up from the washing,
all of them bearing twins
—none of them bereaved.
3 Your lips are like scarlet thread;
your mouth is beautiful;
your cheek is a slice of pomegranate
behind your veil.
4 Your neck is like the tower of David,
built with courses of stones;
a thousand shields are hung upon it
—all the shields of the warriors.
5 Your two breasts are like two fawns,
twin gazelles who graze among the lilies.
6 Until the day comes to life
and the shadows flee,
I will betake myself to the mountain of myrrh
and to the hill of frankincense.
7 You are altogether beautiful, my darling,
and there is no blemish in you.

Recently, I attended a very unusual wedding. It was held on a grassy slope beside the banks of the Allegheny River. Surrounded by beautiful fall colors of orange, russet, and red, under a brilliant blue October sky, we sat and waited for the arrival of the bride. The groom also waited anxiously, scanning the horizon for her appearing. Unlike most brides, this one did not come in a limousine or even on a horse-drawn carriage. Instead, accompanied by violins from the shore, she sailed down the river in a canoe paddled by her father. It was a most unforgettable entrance, and the beginning of a grand celebration.

This picture sets the stage for where we are in the Song of Songs. We have been waiting and waiting throughout the Song, sometimes patiently, sometimes impatiently, for the wedding to be consummated and the bride and the groom to come together, so that their desire for each other can be fulfilled. Now, as we enter this central section of the Song, the waiting is nearly over: it is almost time for the consummation to take place. Before we get there, however, the poet is going to contrast the glory and splendor of Solomon's self-centered palace and extravagant wedding with the simplicity and purity of true love.[1] Money may buy a splendid wedding ceremony in which the camera is focused entirely on you, but money can't buy you love.

Who Is This?

The passage opens with a question: "Who is this coming up from the wilderness . . . ?" (Song 3:6). Many commentators have made the natural—but mistaken—assumption that the answer to the question is to be found in the immediately following verses, which describe King Solomon's glorious bed. As a result, they have imagined a royal procession with a litter (a bed carried by servants) making its way up to Jerusalem from the wilderness, bearing either Solomon himself or the Shulammite inside it. In some cases, as in the ESV, translators have even adjusted the question in the text to match the expected answer, so that the question is rendered: "*What* is that coming up from the wilderness?"[2]

Yet the form of the question is quite clear in Hebrew. It is the same feminine form as the similar question that is asked in Song 6:10 and 8:5, where all translations agree that the answer is the woman. Moreover, a key element in the description of this person coming up from the wilderness is the cloud of scents that accompanies her, especially myrrh and frankincense. There is no mention of any scents associated with Solomon's bed, however. Myrrh and frankincense do not reappear in the poem until the end of the description *of the woman* in 4:1–7, forming an inclusio around this whole section. Once we notice this compositional marker, it is easier to discern the larger structure of the passage: there are two sections in the poem, each of which begins with "Behold!" (or "Wow!," as we might put it more familiarly). The first section describes the fabulous splendor of Solomon's

1. For Solomon's role in the Song as a foil for the image of true love, see Iain M. Duguid, *The Song of Songs: An Introduction and Commentary*, TOTC 19 (Downers Grove, IL: InterVarsity Press, 2015), 35–37.

2. The Hebrew interrogative *mî*, on very rare occasions, can indicate an object rather than a person, but the overwhelming majority of uses are personal ("who?"). For a fuller explanation of the structure of the passage, see Duguid, *The Song of Songs*, 104–5.

isolated, self-protective, and self-centered lifestyle, while the second depicts the unadorned beauty of the woman, whose company is the real treasure and glory of the man who is the hero of the poem.

Solomon's Glory

There is no doubt that Solomon's lifestyle is enviable. To begin with, his bed is an utterly safe place.[3] It is surrounded by no fewer than *sixty* mighty and well-armed warriors, twice the number of his father David's famous personal bodyguard (Song 3:7; see 2 Sam. 23). These warriors are there to provide protection against "terrors of the night" (Song 3:8), which is always a time of risk for people who are potential assassination targets.[4] This image also suggests an interesting contrast with the woman's dream in the previous poem. While she is taking the risk of wandering the streets at night alone, searching desperately for the one whom her soul loves, Solomon is tucked up safely at home, protected from any and all dangers by his overwhelming military might. He is not out enduring the dangers of looking for love because he already has everything he wants.

Of course, if you had a bed like Solomon's, you might want to stay home, too! It is not a simple cot, or a blanket laid over some rushes, of the kind on which poor people might have slept. Rather, it was a bed of extraordinary magnificence, made of wood from Lebanon, with posts of silver, a roof of gold, and a seat of purple. The closest parallels for this level of extravagant opulence in furniture come from the excesses of the Persian king's palace in the book of Esther, where everything is likewise made of gold and precious jewels, as well as the costliest fabrics. This is not a positive point of comparison, for these are, after all, Israel's tax dollars at work. This is especially poignant when we remember that Solomon's high taxation was explicitly mentioned among the political factors that led to the split in the kingdom under Solomon's son Rehoboam (see 1 Kings 12).

The interior of this magnificent bed was also inlaid (or perhaps "paved") with love by the daughters of Jerusalem (Song 3:10). "With love" here could

3. There is nothing to suggest that the bed in verse 7 is coming up from the wilderness; it is safely guarded in Solomon's palace.

4. Some commentators have thought that "terrors of the night" describes night demons familiar from Jewish mythology. Yet against such enemies ordinary swords and training in war would be of little use. The fact that Solomon's bodyguards possess these attributes suggests that more earthly dangers are in view here.

perhaps be taken as an adverbial clause ("lovingly"), describing the devotion to Solomon that prompted the diligence with which the daughters of Jerusalem worked. Alternatively, some have taken "paved with love" as a metaphor describing the sexual interactions between Solomon and the daughters of Jerusalem that take place here.[5] Either way, it is striking that the focus is on the love that the daughters of Jerusalem have for Solomon, and perhaps vice versa, rather than on Solomon's love for his bride or her love for him. If the latter interpretation is correct, then Solomon's lovemaking to the many daughters of Jerusalem in these opulent surroundings contrasts dramatically with the exclusive love of the man and his "darling" (4:1) in the simpler surroundings that the rest of the poem celebrates. In contrast to the bed that belongs to Solomon and the daughters of Jerusalem, the bed of the man and the woman in the poem is not purple but verdantly green, while the beams and rafters of their bed are made not out of gold and silver, but out of simple cedar and pine (1:16–17). While these construction materials may be simple and natural, they nonetheless have an enduring quality that will last long after Solomon's artificial glory has faded away.

Just as the previous two stanzas have focused on Solomon and his substantial entourage, so does the final verse in this section. Here, the daughters of Zion are urged to go out and look at Solomon on his wedding day (Song 3:11). No glances need be spared for his future wife; she is not a central part of the events but rather a mere accessory. Solomon is there in all his splendor, crowned by his mother, with gladness in his heart, yet he appears entirely alone in the center of the spotlight. The reference to Solomon's mother here contrasts with the woman's longing in the previous poem to take her man home to her mother's house, which appears to be a much more humble abode (v. 4). At least on the wedding day of the man and the woman in the poem, though they may lack the glorious outward trimmings of any one of Solomon's many royal weddings, they will share their gladness and joy together, as a couple.

Not Even Solomon in All His Glory . . .

From looking on as an observer to Solomon's wealth and glory, the man then turns his eyes to the true object of his affections, the woman. Now

5. Elie Assis, *Flashes of Fire: A Literary Analysis of the Song of Songs* (New York: T. & T. Clark, 2009), 114.

he no longer has to strain his gaze to discern her in the distance, coming up from the wilderness, the place of waiting and longing, the journey that she has been on for so long. Behold! She is now right in front of him, there for him to feast his eyes on. Fittingly, therefore, he begins his description exactly where he did in chapter 1, with her eyes, which he describes as doves behind her veil (Song 4:1). As before, the focus of this image is inaccessibility, although now the flimsiest of barriers separates them—only a veil, rather than a wall or an inaccessible cliff. Veils were used for a variety of reasons in the ancient Near East, but they were particularly associated with betrothal and weddings, which seems the most likely explanation here. Veils not only separated and divided: they were also used as a symbol of the husband's commitment to provide for his bride, similar to the gesture of covering her with a corner of his garment.[6]

Having begun with her eyes—the most personal and communicative of features—the man does not stop there, as he had at an earlier point in their relationship. Now he allows his eyes to move onward to describe her hair as a flock of black goats, streaming down a mountain (Song 4:1). The image is one of shimmering motion and life. Modern readers, who often live in cities, may have a hard time recognizing this metaphor as a compliment. The woman in the Song, though, was a farm girl who had personal experience with caring for goats (1:8). From goats, we move to sheep, newly shorn and washed, and therefore bright white, each bearing twins. These form an apt analogy for the woman's perfectly matched teeth (4:2). Goats and sheep are a natural pair, as is black and white; the contrasting pairing is strengthened by the fact that the sheep are going up while the goats are coming down.

If the dominant colors in the first strophe are the black goats and white sheep, then the second strophe is dominated by the color red. The woman's lips are like scarlet thread, while her cheeks are like the blush-red halves of a pomegranate (Song 4:3). Pomegranates were associated with fertility on account of their many seeds, a theme never far below the surface of this poem. The unusual word for *mouth* that is used here focuses on its function as the organ of speech (v. 3): it is not merely the appearance of her mouth that is lovely but the words that come from it. Given the fact that the man's

6. Karel van der Toorn, "The Significance of the Veil in the Ancient Near East," in *Pomegranates and Golden Bells: Studies in Biblical, Jewish, and Near Eastern Ritual, Law, and Literature in Honor of Jacob Milgrom*, ed. David P. Wright, David Noel Freedman, and Avi Hurvitz (Winona Lake, IN: Eisenbrauns, 1995), 330–36.

description of the woman is often described as erotic, it is worth noticing how much of the description focuses on the woman's face, and a veiled face at that. In contrast to our pornography-obsessed society, in which everything is revealed and nothing left to the imagination, the Song understands the allure of the hidden. It turns out that modesty can actually be the ultimate in attractiveness after all.

Continuing downward, the woman's neck is compared to the tower of David (Song 4:4). This suggests that she carries herself with a regal and assured bearing, while her neck is also adorned with multilayer necklaces that recall the decorative stonework and different kinds of shields hung about the tower. From the neck, the man's eyes come to rest on her breasts, which he compares to two fawns, the twins of a gazelle, that graze among the lilies (v. 5). As with her teeth, the bodily symmetry of her two breasts allows comparison with twins, once again an image of fertility. This is, of course, particularly apt as an image for the breasts, whose connection with fertility is transparent (see Gen. 49:25). In the Song, however, it is their erotic significance that is primarily in the foreground, as in Proverbs 5:19. Fawns are shy and rarely observed, while gazelles are graceful: both qualities therefore provide a fitting comparison here, as in Proverbs 5:19. Finally, the image of these shy young deer that "graze among the lilies" provides a peaceful pastoral scene of the animals enjoying their natural habitat, feasting on the richest of fare.

As in Song 2:17, the phrase "Until the day comes to life and the shadows flee" (4:6) indicates the long-awaited coming of the morning. Yet whereas in the first passage the woman told the man to turn around and go away, now the time for the consummation of their relationship has finally come. It is time for him to take himself to the mountain of myrrh and the hill of frankincense—the "cleft mountains" of her breasts (2:17)—which are now accessible to his touch. The woman's desire for her beloved to lie between her breasts like a sachet of myrrh all night long (1:13) will finally receive its fulfillment. The clouds of frankincense and myrrh coming up from the wilderness (3:6) envelop him in their sweet perfume as he takes possession of the promised land of her body.

Having described the perfect number (seven) of her "perfect" body parts, it is not surprising that the man concludes his description by saying, "You are altogether beautiful, my darling" (Song 4:7). Not only are the concerns that the woman expressed about her appearance in 1:5 completely swept away, but when he adds "there is no blemish in you" (4:7), the man widens his affirmation of her beauty beyond merely her physical appearance to every aspect of her personality (see Dan. 1:4). The man's comprehensive delight in his bride is thus comparable to the Lord's delight in his original creation when he surveyed all that he had made and declared that it was "very good" (Gen. 1:31).

Two Competing Models of Love

In Song 3:6–4:8, we have two contrasting and competing views of what love and marriage are about. On the one hand, we have Solomon's version of love and marriage that is thoroughly self-centered. It is all about him. As we can see from 1 Kings 11, Solomon accumulated numerous wives and concubines, not necessarily because he was a sexual addict, but because there were specific things that he hoped they would accomplish for him. Numerous wives meant security and significance for Solomon in a variety of ways. The alliances that would be forged by marrying the daughters of the kings of the surrounding nations were viewed as a means to political security and economic prosperity. In addition, multiplying wives and concubines meant the potential to have far more offspring than one wife could ever provide, again providing a kind of security, since members of the extensive royal family would come to dominate key positions of influence and power. There would also be little prospect of not having a male heir to continue the dynasty, ensuring that the line of David would have an ongoing legacy.

There is a sense in which Solomon's strategy seemed to be working for him, as we can see in the poem. He acquired astonishing wealth and splendor, a glory that is (not coincidentally) visibly portrayed in the opulence of his bed. He was perfectly safe at night, surrounded by his overwhelming bodyguard. As we know from the book of 1 Kings, he had many children and was succeeded on his throne by his own son Rehoboam. Yet in pursuing this vision of "love" and marriage, he is depicted entirely alone in the center of the spotlight in all his splendor. The strategy may have been working for him, but it didn't have to work for his wives: they were primarily objects that enabled him to reach his real goals. In seeking out the treasures and security of this world, he missed a pearl of greater price, namely, the simple joy of true love. And where does God fit into his vision of life? Could not God guard him from all danger and provide him with an heir, as he had promised (2 Sam. 7:12–16)? In seeking to use "love" to manage all the risks out of his life, Solomon had already turned his back on trusting the Lord, long before his numerous foreign wives led him astray to worship other gods.

In striking contrast, the man in the poem has a very different vision of love and marriage. This couple have no bodyguards to protect them from the dangers of the night, which means that they have both the need and the opportunity to find their refuge in the Lord. The man is counting on this one woman to have the fertility that is necessary for his family line and influence to continue, a strategy that—based on the experience of other biblical characters—required him to trust and pray for the Lord, who is the true source of all fertility, to open her womb (cf. Gen. 25:21). They may have had little wealth or splendor of which to boast, but they had a greater treasure than Solomon in all his glory: they had each other.

Love and Idolatry

We, too, are often driven in our evaluation of potential relationship candidates by the Solomonic concerns for security and significance. We choose a partner on the basis of what we believe that person can do for us rather than because of a true love that is drawn to who he or she truly is. In our culture, most of us don't have arranged marriages in which political and financial matters take priority. It is also true that the safety and financial provision that in the past women looked for in a man can now be pursued through a career, not just through marriage. Yet the temptation for us to view our relationships through the lens of what they can do for us surely has not changed. We believe that *this* person and *this* relationship will provide for us the security and significance that we so desperately seek.

Of course, the security and significance that we desire comes in many different shapes and sizes. We may feel safe and significant simply because now we have a relationship. If our idolatry is simply of a relationship itself, we are likely to enter relationships without really knowing the other person, stay in dysfunctional relationships when it is evident to everyone else that they are going nowhere, and rush from one relationship to the next because we cannot bear the prospect of being alone. We may be abused or neglected by our spouse or lover, but at least we have a relationship, which is really what matters to us.

Alternatively, we may feel significant simply because the person that we are in relationship with is physically attractive. In that case, we may neglect the fact that we can never have a real conversation or interact with this person on a deep heart level because what really matters is that we look good together. Of course, there are some very attractive people who are not at all shallow, and unattractive people who have no substance. The issue is what draws us to this person: is it simply appearance, or something more substantive? Or perhaps we enter a relationship because we are looking for the father that we never had in our relationship. In this case, we want someone who will make all the decisions for us and tell us what to think and what to do. That feels safe for us.

For myself, when I was in college I exuded insecurity. I desperately wanted to feel safe in a relationship and feared rejection deeply. The person that I was in a relationship with was less important than the fact that someone—anyone—felt that I measured up. As a result, any relationships that I managed to initiate tended to die fairly quickly, strangled by my own insecurity. My relationships were far more about me than they were about the other person. Indeed, I still struggle with that self-centered desire for approval in all my relationships.

The common factor in all of this is that we "love" the other person because of something that he or she can do for us. Sometimes that approach may seem to "work" for us, as Solomon's idolatries did for him. We may find the security and significance that we crave in this person. In that case, we will be happy and content with our lot. At other times, in the mercy of God, the relationship may be a deep disappointment to us as the other person proves unwilling or unable to fulfill our prescribed agenda. In that case, we will often grow angry and resentful toward the person, or even toward God, because of our deep disappointment. We may go through a sequence of unsuccessful relationships, every time looking for something that we cannot find, because we are looking for it in the wrong place. Either way, whether our idols of love are blessing or cursing us, we judge the relationship a success or a failure based on what we get out of the other person.

Captivated by Her

In contrast to the Solomonic model, in which the spotlight shines with undivided attention on Solomon alone, the man in the poem has his eyes entirely fixed on his spouse-to-be. He is captivated by her beauty: he finds her overwhelmingly, entrancingly attractive. Nor is it just her physical beauty that attracts him. The speech of her mouth and the strength of character evident in the way she holds herself are also attractive to him. He shines the spotlight entirely on her and delights in who she is. Meanwhile, as we will see in a later chapter, she shines it right back at him. The back-and-forth of mutual praise that we saw in chapter 1, which is echoed in his opening words, is the common thread running through the story of their love. She thereby becomes a true partner with him in building a lasting and loving house together—a house that may lack Solomon's material wealth and vast progeny but that has a splendor of its own that Solomon in all his glory cannot match. On this model, marriage is two people's becoming one flesh: a single unit that rises and falls together, and that sticks together for better or for worse, for richer or for poorer, in sickness or in health, till death parts them. She submits to him as the church submits to Christ; he gives himself for her as Christ gives himself for the church (Eph. 5:24–25).

The only way to make this kind of other-centered commitment to a spouse, of course, is to find your security and significance somewhere other than in that person. As long as your spouse is your idol, you will need that person too much to be able to serve him or her well. You will place a heavy burden of expectation on your spouse to fulfill your needs, a burden that he or she will never be able to bear and may well come to resent. Meanwhile, your spouse may be placing his or her own expectations on you. That pathway, with which every relationship will struggle to some degree or another, leads to conflict and disharmony, as you each seek to use the other person to serve yourself. Marriage becomes a competitive sport with winners and losers, rather than a team event in which you work together to serve each other.

But if you begin to find your security and significance in the Lord, you will start to be freed to delight in the unique ways in which the Lord has gifted your spouse and fitted her or him for you. Perhaps your beloved's shining features are not hair like a flock of goats and a neck like the tower of David but her fair skin and her dazzling smile. Maybe there is a reason why the man in the poem doesn't mention the woman's nose here (though he will in chapter 7)! Yet he delights in her features and her character and celebrates the one whom he is about to marry and to whom he will commit his life forever. He isn't just in love with being in love; he is in love with *her.* The terms he uses to describe her body show that he anticipates this marriage as being a movement for both of them from an arid wilderness to a promised land—a fertile, lush, and fruitful environment that is filled with every blessing.

Methinks He Doth Delight Too Much?

Does the expectation and anticipation of joy in this passage seem a little overblown to you? Maybe it doesn't, if you are not yet married. Perhaps you anticipate your marriage as being a permanent paradise of pleasures, a constant garden of delights, in which each day is better than the one before. It is true that marriage can be great, with many pleasures and delights. It is a wonderful blessing and gift of God. Yet marriage can also be very hard and painful, as two sinners crash against each other, bruising and wounding each other with their competing idolatries. There may be times when that beautiful regal bearing actually appears to you more like stiff-necked obstinacy, and when that delightful mouth utters hurtful and harsh words. There may also be times when you hurt her in ways that you did not think yourself capable of, bringing hot tears to those dovelike eyes. In reality, even in the best of marriages you will discover that she is not "altogether beautiful" and without flaw—and neither are you. We are all deeply broken: idolaters to the core.

Yet this hyperbolic language, which we are most tempted to use on the day of our wedding to the one whom our soul loves, is actually intended to lift our gaze beyond any human relationship. Marriage, even the best of marriages, doesn't really transport the bride from the wilderness to the promised land. Even though on her wedding day the bride may look radiantly beautiful—in some cases, almost unrecognizable from her usual "jeans and T-shirt" attire—she is still the same sinner underneath, and so is the groom. Only one marriage can effect such a radical change in our status, clothing us in an imputed perfection and bringing us into a new and enduring inheritance. In only one marriage are our needs for security and significance met at a deep and satisfying level: the marriage of Jesus Christ and his true bride, the church.

The Marriage for Which We Long

Our heaven-made match with Jesus Christ is a marriage in which the groom was not by any means "all about himself." Even though Jesus was physically descended from the line of David through Solomon, and was therefore of royal descent, he did not come to earth to acquire a fortune and assert his status. On the contrary, Jesus said, "Foxes have holes, and birds of the air have nests, but the Son of Man has nowhere to lay his head" (Matt. 8:20). He did not come to be served himself but to serve others, loving and caring for them even when he was tired and weary from a long day of ministry. He was not safely protected at night by sixty armed men against any and all dangers. On the contrary, Jesus came to give his life as a ransom for many, submitting to the pain and ignominy of the cross in order to free us from the eternal death that we deserved. The Good Shepherd came to lay down his life for his sheep (John 10:11).

In this act of self-sacrifice, Jesus was fulfilling a long history of the one-sided relationship between the Lord and his people, in which the Lord loved and cared for the children of Israel and they spurned him in favor of their idols. So, for example, the Lord sent the prophet Hosea to act out the story of his love for his people by loving a prostitute, Gomer. Even though she was persistently faithless and abandoned him, following a lifestyle that took her out into the wilderness, Hosea was told to go after her and win her back, continually showing love to her among the shattered ruins of her life.

Here is where your true security and significance may be found. The God of the universe so loved you that he sent his only Son to come into this world and die for you. You matter to him. He cares for you, even though you have not cared for him and have run from him, perhaps finding yourself today in a spiritual wilderness far from home. His gaze is nonetheless fixed on you, not just as one human being out of a teeming mass of humanity, but as an individual creation of his hands. As the psalmist said, "You knitted me together in my mother's womb" (Ps. 139:13). The Lord chose your hair, whether it is a like a flock of unruly goats or barely there at all anymore. He painted the color in your cheeks, gave you your teeth, and assigned you your body shape. He created your personality, with all its quirks and charms. If you are a Christian, he is at work in you by his Holy Spirit, remaking you into a new creation whose final splendor and glory will be a dazzling thing of wonder for all eternity. God loves you!

Do you see how that reality frees you genuinely to love others, whether you are married or single? You, too, are a broken sinner with Solomonic strivings to use love to serve your own agenda. Yet God's love is what assures you that you matter in this world. His care is forever. He will never leave you or forsake you. You are secure in him. The more you grasp this truth, the less you will need to milk these things out of your relationships. You will be set free actually to serve those around you: your spouse, your children, and your friends. Rooted and grounded in God's love, you can finally enter relationships not for what people can do for you but in order to show that same love to them.

Perhaps you have never entered that one relationship with God through Jesus Christ. He invites you to come to him now, broken and messed up as you may be, perhaps with a string of broken relationships behind you. He invites you to come, bow down your heart before him, and enter into the love that he has for you. Receive the grace and forgiveness that he offers you in Jesus.

Or perhaps you are a believer in Jesus, yet you can see that your current relationships are a mess of sin and selfishness and Solomonic striving. You, too, need to return to Christ's love for you. Behold, Jesus is altogether beautiful, perfect, and without blemish. Yet for you he entered this wilderness of a world and became nothing, until at the cross his beauty was marred beyond all human recognition. His hands were pierced by sharp nails; his side thrust through by a cruel spear; his face twisted by physical and spiritual agony, topped not with a bridal wreath but with a mocking crown of thorns. In Jesus Christ, the God of all glory fixed his gaze on you, in all your personal spiritual ugliness, and through Christ's death in your place, he has now clothed you in Christ's perfect beauty. All his perfect relationships are credited to you, so that you are declared to be absolutely without blemish in him. By his grace, mercy, and love, one day God will make you into an unblemished lover, when he takes you to be with himself, and even now he is growing your ability to love as he loves. Oh, for that day to come, when the darkness and shadows flee, and we can gaze on his beauty forever! There in Christ is the true treasure for which you have been searching your whole life, the true security in which we may deeply rest. There in Christ is your life, forever.

7

Consummation

Song of Songs 4:8—5:1

Man
8 [Come] with me from Lebanon, bride, come from Lebanon.
Travel from the peak of Amana,
from the peak of Senir and Hermon,
from the dens of lions,
from the mountains of leopards.
9 You have stolen my heart, my sister and bride,
you have stolen my heart with one [glance] from your eyes,
one strand from your necklace.
10 How delightful are your caresses, my sister and bride
—how much better are your caresses than wine,
and the scent of your oils than all spices.
11 Your lips drip nectar, bride;
honey and milk are under your tongue,
and the fragrance of your garments is like the fragrance of Lebanon.
12 A locked garden is my sister-bride,
an enclosed fountain, a sealed spring.
13 Your shoots are a paradise of pomegranates,
with choice fruits—henna and nard.
14 Nard and saffron, calamus and cinnamon, with every incense tree,
myrrh and aloes, with all the best perfumes.

[15] A garden spring, a well of living water,
flowing streams from Lebanon.

Woman
[16] Arouse, O north [wind] and go in, O south [wind]!
Blow on my garden;
let its perfumes flow!
Let my beloved come in to his garden
so that he may eat its choice fruits.

Man
[5:1] I come to my garden, my sister and bride.
I pluck my myrrh with my spices;
I eat my honeycomb with my honey;
I drink my wine with my milk.

Daughters of Jerusalem
Eat, friends, drink, and get drunk with caresses.

And so to bed. Or rather, "And so to wed." Or more precisely still, both together. This three-stanza poem at the very heart of the Song explores and extols the intimate and God-designed connection between marriage and sex. It is not coincidental that the third stanza of this poem (Song 4:16–5:1), with its celebration of the delights of married love, forms the exact center of the Song, with 111 lines before it (excluding the superscription) and 111 lines after it.[1] This structure makes it a very countercultural poem in a culture where we treat sexual desire just like any other biological appetite. Yet its emphasis on marriage as a garden of sexual delight was equally countercultural in its ancient context, which often regarded marriage as a means to the end of political and financial security, or simply as a method of controlling lust and producing progeny. As a result, this poem is countercultural in virtually every culture around the world: biblical wisdom almost always runs against the grain.

The fundamental reality of every culture is that we are deeply broken people at the core of our beings, and so we will inevitably twist and destroy everything that God has made good. Although the original sin was *not* sex

1. G. Lloyd Carr, *The Song of Solomon: An Introduction and Commentary*, TOTC 17 (Downers Grove, IL: InterVarsity Press, 1984), 127.

or lust, that first rebellion against God in the garden of Eden immediately and deeply affected our sexuality. The first man and woman's state of being naked and unashamed together was destroyed by the fall, so that they felt the need to cover themselves immediately with fig leaves (Gen. 3:7). What God made good, sin turned into shame. That lasting legacy continues on into our own experience of sexuality. We may feel the shame of sin in many different dimensions of our lives, but our sexuality is surely one of the most frequent areas in which we feel ashamed. What God made good, we have spoiled.

This poem takes something that we have ruined and shows us with breathtaking beauty what the proper expression of our sexuality ought to look like. Its motivation is to stir our desire for purity and joy. In so doing, however, it cannot help but expose the reality that we all fall far short in this area. In this way, our broken sexuality drives us back once again to see all the more clearly our desperate need for the gospel.

Coming from the Wilderness

As with the previous poem, the woman is pictured at the outset in a dangerous and remote wilderness. In this case, it is the distant mountain ranges of Lebanon, the lair of dangerous wild animals and the home of exotic spices (Song 4:8). This theme of the woman's being visible but inaccessible has appeared before in the poem, for example, when the man described her as a dove among the crannies of the cliff (2:14). Once again he invites her to come with him on a journey. This time, however, instead of asking her to leave the safety of home to go into the risky outdoors of premarital sex, he is calling her to join him on a journey from a dangerous wilderness to the safe delight of a lush garden. What is more, this time he will receive a different answer to his request.

It is significant, too, that in this poem he calls her *bride* for the first time. The word occurs no fewer than six times in this poem (Song 4:8, 9, 10, 11, 12; 5:1) and nowhere else in the Song, emphatically connecting the sexual experience described here with the legal status that goes with it. This word can hardly simply be a metaphor, as some commentators have sought to make it. In what context would an unmarried couple use such a term as a metaphor in any culture, ancient or modern?[2] Elsewhere in the Bible, the

2. Richard S. Hess, *Song of Songs*, BCOTWP (Grand Rapids: Baker Academic, 2005), 139n61.

word always indicates the new familial bond that is brought into existence through marriage, and its use here in the Song marks a key turning point in the couple's relationship. Marriage creates the legal and relational context in which it is right and appropriate for the locked garden to be unlocked and the sealed fountain to be unsealed.

Yet their bond is not simply legal. It is also an affectionate bond of companionship. She is not merely his bride but his sister. This is where the language turns metaphorical, using a term of endearment well attested in ancient Near Eastern love poetry. She is not *literally* his sister. Rather, the word indicates that the friendship in their marriage is like that between a brother and a sister, the closest bond that was possible with a person of the opposite gender in antiquity. In chapter 8, the woman will wish that the man were her brother so that she could openly display her love for him (Song 8:1). It is a reminder that legal and sexual union were never intended to exist by themselves. When the man and the woman in Genesis 2:24 became one flesh in the original marriage, it indicated much more than mere physical intimacy. It is a union of body and soul, in which two people are united in every aspect of their lives. From then on, they are no longer two separate individuals but rather one new body, in which mutual care, companionship, respect, and self-giving are the logical consequence (see Eph. 5:28–30).

You Have Captured My Heart

Yet while their relationship is more than sexual, it is certainly not less than sexual. The man passionately craves the woman. The phrase "You have stolen my heart" (Song 4:9) means something different in Hebrew than it does in English. In the West, we think with our heads and feel with our hearts. As a result, we call someone who has lost his ability to love *heartless*, while an unthinking reaction is *mindless*. In Hebrew, however, the heart is where you think, so the person who has lost his heart is a person who cannot think straight, someone who in our parlance has "lost his head." In effect, the man is saying, "You drive me out of my mind." This is the mirror image of the woman's earlier declaration that she is "sick with love" (2:5). Once again his attention is drawn to her eyes and her jeweled necklace (4:9). The metaphorical weapons with which her neck is surrounded have been successfully used against him and have captured him completely. The man is a prisoner of love.

Such a self-revelation is far riskier than the rich compliments of the previous section. You may admire someone's attractiveness in a flirtatious way from a safe distance, but a declaration about your heart is a statement of personal commitment that requires either acceptance or rejection. In other words, you can respond to "You look cute in that outfit" with a simple "Thank you." But if someone says to you, "You drive me out of my mind," that requires something more than "Oh, thanks." It is a dangerous, self-revealing declaration of love that must be either received or refused.[3]

In the beginning of the Song, it was the woman's desire that sought the fulfillment of a kiss. Now, in an expression of the mutuality of true love, the man feels what she first felt. Now it is *her* caresses that are better than wine (Song 4:10; see 1:2–3). Yet the comparison of the lovers' bodies to vineyards in between these two declarations enhances and enriches the metaphor, since wine is the product of a vineyard that has been long protected against the depredations of the little foxes and is now in full fruit. Having waited faithfully, the couple now find their love in full flower, ready to be consummated.

A Paradise of Pomegranates

As in the opening chapter, fragrance and taste go back and forth as the dominant senses. The fragrance of Lebanon, a common symbol in the Old Testament for a land blossoming with prosperity, combines with the presence of honey and milk under the woman's tongue to evoke a comparison between her and the Promised Land.[4] Like the Promised Land, her body becomes a symbol of complete prosperity, fruitfulness, and rest. The phrase "Your lips drip nectar" (Song 4:11) exactly parallels Proverbs 5:3, where it describes the kiss of the adulterous woman. True delight and satisfaction are actually to be found in the arms of the bride, not in the embrace of an amorous stranger.

Yet this time, the couple will not stop merely with kisses! As their relationship reaches its climax, the man describes the woman as she has been

3. See Carey Ellen Walsh, *Exquisite Desire: Religion, the Erotic, and the Song of Songs* (Minneapolis: Fortress, 2000), 75.

4. See Ellen F. Davis, "Romance of the Land in the Song of Songs," *ATR* 80 (1998): 533–46.

up until this point: she is a locked garden and a sealed fountain (Song 4:12). In those days, kings and wealthy people created gardens as private places of leisure and intimacy with privileged friends. Such places were not open to be viewed or trampled by the general public. Likewise, in an arid climate, fountains were used to provide the water that was necessary for a garden to produce its lush growth. Such precious water could not be freely distributed to all without depriving the garden of its resources, and so it was sealed.

The images of a fountain and flowing water are used to describe both male and female sexuality in Proverbs 5:15–19, which says:

> Drink water from your own cistern,
> flowing water from your own well.
> Should your springs be scattered abroad,
> streams of water in the streets?
> Let them be for yourself alone,
> and not for strangers with you.
> Let your fountain be blessed,
> and rejoice in the wife of your youth,
> a lovely deer, a graceful doe.
> Let her breasts fill you at all times with delight;
> be intoxicated always in her love.

This lyric makes it clear that there is no double standard: both men and women alike are to restrain their sexual desire until and within marriage. This is not because God is harsh and restrictive, or has imposed laws designed to prevent human flourishing. Quite the contrary: such restraint is the precise means whereby the delightful fruitfulness, unique intimacy, and glorious rest that a sexual relationship was designed to bring can be fulfilled.

The image of the sexual relationship as a locked garden containing innumerable delights evokes the recollection of the original walled garden, Eden itself, where the Lord met daily with Adam and Eve. Like the original garden, the woman's body is literally a paradise (Song 4:13; Heb. *pardis*, though this exact word is never used of Eden)—filled with every good fruit and aromatic spice. Every spice that is mentioned elsewhere in the Song is present in this garden. Its products come from many different lands and include common henna along with exotic spikenard and saffron. No literal garden could possibly have sustained all these different plants, which simply heightens the Edenic associations.

As the poem progresses, the focus of the images of a garden and a fountain shifts from representing the woman's virginal purity to her identity as the source of abundant and rich life. She is a luxuriant *garden* and a *well* flowing with cool streams of living water. What is being celebrated here is not perpetual virginity and abstinence, but rather a sexual purity that leads to and supports a fruitful and delightful union in marriage.

The woman joyfully responds to the man's words by inviting him to come to his garden and enjoy its choice fruits (Song 4:16). The garden that had been locked and the fountain that was sealed are now freely and eagerly opened up for him to enjoy. When she summons north and south winds to "arouse" her garden, she uses the same verb that she used earlier when she warned the daughters of Jerusalem against arousing love too soon (see 2:7; 3:5; 8:4). The winds turn the formerly slumbering and locked garden into an opened and awakened paradise that wafts abroad its fragrance when the long-awaited day of union finally arrives. She is ready for the man to enter the garden of her body and enjoy its delights.

I Come to My Garden

The man is equally eager to accept her invitation. Now she is no longer simply "a garden"; she is "my garden" (Song 5:1). In fact, there are no fewer than eight first-person-singular possessives in verse 1 in the course of a mere sixteen Hebrew words, emphasizing the exclusiveness of their marital relationship. Now the myrrh and spices, the honeycomb and honey, the wine and milk that he described in the preceding verses belong to him and him alone to enjoy. At this moment of consummation, he describes her once again as "my sister and bride," expressing the delightful relational and legal intimacy that provides the safe context for the sexual intimacy that they will now share. The family wall that separated them in 2:9 has been bridged with the creation of a new family unit: she has left her father and mother and been joined to her husband, and the two have become one flesh (Gen. 2:24).

At this central and climactic moment of the poem, an unidentified speaker adds words of approbation: "Eat, friends, drink and get drunk with caresses!" (Song 5:1). Whether the speaker is the daughters of Jerusalem, the wider community, or God himself giving his sanction on the couple's union is ultimately unimportant. Whoever is speaking reflects the author's evaluation of the consummation of their marriage, declaring it to be "very good." Yet these words remind us once again that sex and marriage are not simply the private satisfaction of individual appetites and pleasures between consenting adults but always exist in the larger context of the community of faith.

The Glory of Purity

What does this beautiful poem have to teach us in our sex-saturated society? To begin with, it clearly holds out as its ideal remaining chaste before marriage and monogamous within marriage. This is, of course, the church's traditional teaching, which is far removed from what many non-Christians believe today. Sex is for marriage, and for marriage alone—and marriage is for one man and one woman. That is how God created it in the first place in the garden of Eden with Adam and Eve, and it remains how it is intended to be, forever and ever.

As we noted in chapter 3, however, the way in which the Song argues for this position is very different from the way in which the church often argues for chastity and monogamy. Instead of focusing on the biblical commands not to commit adultery or not to pursue premarital or same-sex relationships, it paints a picture of the beauty of biblical marriage. Both approaches may reflect biblical wisdom, of course. The commands are no less biblical than the beautiful portrait. It is appropriate for churches to teach clearly that lust, premarital sex, adultery, homosexual sex, and unbiblical divorce are wrong, just as Jesus and Paul did (e.g., Matt. 5:27–28; 19:3–9; Rom. 1:18–32; 1 Cor. 6:18; Eph. 5:3). Yet alongside that, if we are to be true to the biblical witness, we also need to show people the glorious attractiveness of what biblical marriage was intended to be. This passage is, if you like, God's "You may surely eat of every tree of the garden" that accompanies and precedes the prohibition "but of the tree of the knowledge of good and evil you shall not eat" (Gen. 2:16–17).

God is not against sex. He invented sex, with all the intense physical and emotional pleasures that it brings. He deliberately designed all the intricate organs, nerves, and blood vessels that make sex so enticing. Yet he invented it not as a freestyle sport but as a powerful bonding agent within a marital relationship, in which the legal and relational bonds designed to support it are there as well. It is the sister-bride whose garden the man desires to enter. These three things—the legal, the affectionate, and the sexual—are designed to belong together. Remove any one, and you have a deformed relationship.

That is not hard to see, if we view the matter properly. For example, if you remove the affectionate component from the relationship, as many traditional cultures do, you have legal marriage and sex without love and intimacy. At worst, that is legalized rape. Even at best, though, it is a travesty of what marriage and sex were designed to be, turning them into a selfish exercise of sexual conquest, in which the person is used as an object to achieve selfish ends. For example, in some traditional cultures around the world, a woman must prove her fertility to be a good candidate for marriage, and infertility is considered just grounds for divorce, since the primary goal of having a wife is to produce offspring.

It is perhaps easy for us to see that marriage without affection is a deformed relationship, since we have a very different view in our culture. In our context, however, we have plenty of sex without love and intimacy *or* legal marriage—casual "hooking up" with someone that we just met and have no intention of getting to know or to marry. The same is true of the widespread use of pornography or romantic-fantasy literature. When we fantasize sexually about an actor or actress, or even a person that we know, there is neither a legal relationship nor any real intimacy. It is as plastic and fake as a shop-window mannequin. Yet many of us are pouring our sexuality into such fantasies, in which there is no real connection with anyone other than ourselves. In some cases, it is the excitement of the sexual high itself that we crave. In others, we are using sex to fill in a void in our lives: to achieve a sense of intimacy, power, or security, or to numb the pain of loneliness, failure, or an empty life.

The Bible's response to such casual misuse of our sexuality is not merely to say, "That's wrong! Don't do it. You'll either get pregnant or go blind!" Rather, it says to us, "How incredibly sad to take something as precious and beautiful as sex and reduce it to mere physicality! How tragic to take a beautiful garden that God has stocked with every delightful flower and spice and allow it to be trampled down flat until our hearts become as hard and cold as a parking lot. What a terrible waste of something that God made so glorious!"

Yet the Bible tells us that for our sexuality to flourish, not only do we need relational intimacy, we also need to be legally bonded to a life partner. That point, which is self-evident in traditional cultures, is much harder to make in our context. Why do we need *marriage* in order to have sex, provided that we have true love? If I love her and she loves me and we have a great relationship, why do I need a piece of paper to validate that before we sleep together? What has society to do with what consenting adults do in their own bedrooms?

There are a number of valid reasons why society has a legitimate interest in sex and marriage. Here, though, I simply want to point out why God has an interest in this area for those who claim to be his children. Why does God care whether you have made a public commitment in marriage before you sleep with your boyfriend or girlfriend? The answer is that there is a crucial difference between a relationship in which you say, "I love you right now, and if anything changes I'll let you know" and one in which you say, "I love you and commit to you forever: in sickness and in health, for richer or for poorer, for better, for worse: till death do us part." God designed sex to operate in a relationship in which there is a clear, lasting, lifelong commitment to the other person. Only in that context is there enough safety to let loose the power of your sexuality, which is designed to bond you permanently to the other person. With sex, you take a lot of risks and make yourself extremely vulnerable to the other person. To do that in anything less than a permanent relationship is like taking a piece of tape and sticking it onto something, then unsticking it, then resticking it, and then unsticking it again. The end result is that the tape loses its power to bond properly to anything. God intended marriage to be a permanent bond, and for sex to be experienced within that safe, loving context—a context analogous to the safety of God's permanent, unbreakable love for us.

Finally, if these ideas are true, then even a relationship in which you have both the legal and the affectionate parts is incomplete without the sexual. Of course, in every marriage there are times and seasons when sex has to be put on hold; as Paul reminded the Corinthians, however, that should be for just a season, not permanent abstinence (1 Cor. 7:5). Augustine's ideal of celibate marriage is far from the biblical ideal, in which men and women were intended to find in their spouse's body a garden of passionate delights. Yet many marriages, even good Christian marriages, experience challenges and disappointments in this area. Purity before marriage is not an automatic guarantee of a great sex life within marriage, as though God owed some recompense for your obedience. The Song itself addresses some of these issues in the next poem, but if this is an area of struggle within your marriage, I encourage you to reach out and seek help. Don't simply assume that marriage plus affection equals great sex. Study the subject and learn to excel at it. If particular emotional or physiological issues make this a challenging area of your marriage, get counseling and assistance. Sex was intended by God to be a delightful and fun part of the marriage relationship!

The Guilt of Impurity

By this point in the Song, some readers may be feeling considerable guilt and shame because they have not protected their purity. Their garden has not been locked and their spring has not been sealed. Many of us have pursued sexual satisfaction outside the context of legal and affectionate relationships, and have fallen far short of God's standards. For some, the struggle might be the addictive use of pornography; for others, it might be same-sex attraction. Still others might not technically have had sex, perhaps, but have done anything and everything else. That is hardly surprising, given the combination of our own desperately fallen natures, the sex-saturated society in which we live, and the skill of the evil one in matching temptation to our personal temperament. Some were exposed to pornography or abused at a young age by those whom they trusted. Others may have no such "excuse" but still know from bitter experience the intense weakness of their own souls. You did not choose the desires with which you wrestle. Perhaps you think you are the only one who wrestles in this way because you have never shared your struggle with anyone else. If so, welcome into the light of God's truth. You are not alone but are surrounded by many fellow strugglers; you are part of a band of sexually broken brothers and sisters.

Some people, however, possibly feel quite proud of their personal purity. If so, have you forgotten what Jesus said in the Sermon on the Mount about lust (Matt. 5:27–28)? You might not have physically engaged in sex, but have you imagined yourself in steamy romantic or sexual relationships, whether with members of the opposite sex or the same sex? Or perhaps you are completely uninterested in sex, which, so far from being a sign of great holiness, could simply be a different form of brokenness. There is no one who can measure up to the glorious picture of this bride and groom on their wedding day, not even one.

The Remedy for Our Guilt and Pride

This is why we so desperately need the relationship toward which human marriage points: the relationship between Christ and the church. The goal of the Song of Songs is not simply to teach God's people how to have great sex within marriage. Rather, the Song gives us a glimpse into the heart of the God who himself loves us so passionately. For that reason, all three elements of a great human marriage point to Christ's relationship with us in their own way.

First, there is the legal aspect. When Jesus Christ calls you to himself, he doesn't just say to you, "I love you for now; let's see how this works out as we go along. If you are holy enough and devout enough over the next fifty years or so, then maybe I'll take you to heaven when you die." No! When God calls you to himself, he legally binds himself to you in a covenant relationship, permanently and unbreakably. Those whom God chose before the foundation of the world he calls into a relationship with himself; those whom he calls he also justifies; those whom he justifies he sanctifies; and those whom he sanctifies he will take to be with him forever (cf. Rom. 8:29–30). The security of your salvation does not rest, therefore, on the strength of your vow to follow Jesus; rather, it rests on his initial and irrevocable choice. Those sheep that the Father has given to the Son no one can snatch from his hands (John 10:28–29). If you belong to Christ, the Holy Spirit will enable you to persevere by faith until the very end. When you truly put your faith in Christ, it is a legal bond, for better or for worse, in sickness and in health, for richer or for poorer, that not even death can dissolve.

But Jesus' relationship with you is not merely legal; it is also deeply affectionate. God is not just stuck with you forever, as if you both had too much to drink in Las Vegas and made a bad decision while passing a drive-through wedding chapel. God actually loves you, hard though that may be for us to grasp sometimes! He knows you inside and out, with all your quirks and weaknesses, all your habitual sins and your heart idolatries, and yet he still loves you personally. God reveals his heart of love for you on the pages of

Scripture and desires that you come to know and love him in the same way that he already knows and loves you.

God is not simply fond of you, in the way that you may be fond of your little brother. What is it that sex is intended by God to add to marriage, beyond mere companionship and friendship? It is fire! Sex is all about deep passion and unique commitment. That is why we crave it so much, because it persuades us that we matter intensely to someone. Love is a flaming fire, as we will see later on in the Song. The burning love that we see in our sexuality is a picture of the passionate intensity of the love that God has for us.

God's Fiery Love

Nothing less than such an intense, burning love could ever explain the cross. A mild fondness for humanity would not have been enough to propel the infinite, glorious God of all creation to humble himself to the point of taking on flesh and becoming a mere mortal. Why would the Eternal One enter time and take on all the limitations of our tiny form? Burning love. Why would the Holy One enter a sinful world and befriend deeply broken sinners? Burning love. Because of his passionate yearning for us, Jesus Christ bore the frustrations of life in this fallen world, where he was constantly surrounded by people who failed him and let him down.

Ultimately, the people whom Jesus loved betrayed him. God's own people, whom he had faithfully been wooing throughout the Old Testament, rejected his Messiah, choosing to have a terrorist released instead of Jesus (see Mark 15:7–15). They then conspired with the Romans to nail Jesus to the cross, where he would endure hours of indescribable physical agony and pain. The worst pain, however, was the spiritual pain of bearing mountains of our sin—yours and mine—including all the sexual sin that we have thought and acted out. The Jews and the Romans weren't the only ones to betray Jesus. We betrayed him, too, and continue to do so, day after day after day. Our mountains of sin and betrayal were laid on his shoulders, for which he experienced the burning wrath of the Father that must have scorched his very soul.

What did it cost the Father, too, to bruise the Son like that? The Father was not standing by impassively pouring out his wrath on Jesus. Every wound that the Son received must have caused the Father to flinch. Every blow that struck Jesus was measured out to him by the Father with whom he had shared unbroken fellowship and intimacy since before the universe began. What human father could endure the pain of seeing his beloved child suffer like that? What human husband would bear such pain and shame for the sake of his bride? What earthly lover would endure such ignominy for a beloved who had repeatedly shown herself to be so unworthy and unfaithful? There is not one. There is only one Father and Husband and Lover like that: the God who created us for himself and who will not let us go. The Father who now sees us united to his Son delights to gaze on us with the same intensity with which he delights in his own Son. Jesus Christ loved his bride and gave himself for her, so that she could be presented to him on her wedding day pure and spotless, clothed in a righteousness that she didn't earn, without blemish. He didn't marry us because we were beautiful: he married us in order to make us beautiful by the power of his transforming love.

This is the God who calls you to mirror that same intense, burning, committed love in your relationships. He calls you to chastity as long as you are unmarried: chastity in your mind as well as in your actions. He calls you to sexual faithfulness within marriage, not just abstaining from sex in all its wrong forms but properly delighting in sex as the gift that it was intended to be, a wonderful gift that you can give to your spouse and that your spouse can give to you. God calls you to show to a watching world the kind of permanent, unbreakable, legal bond that is at the very same time filled with tender affection and great passion, true friendship on fire.

Our sexuality is at best merely a faint reflection of the true marriage that we are all called to celebrate, whether we are single, married, divorced, or widowed. We have all failed and fallen short in our sexuality, and may properly feel ashamed and guilty of our sin. Yet Jesus comes to us with a word of forgiveness rather than condemnation. People once brought to Jesus a woman who had been taken in the very act of adultery (John 8:3): there was no question about her sin, just as there is perhaps no question in your heart about your own sin, even if no one else knows about it. Jesus said to the crowd, "Let him who is without sin among you be the first to throw a stone" (v. 7). Gradually, one by one, the crowd turned and went away. Yet still the woman was not safe. There was One there who was without sin, who could righteously have condemned her to death, who could have cast the first stone. But he didn't. Instead, Jesus said, "Neither do I condemn you; go, and from now on sin no more" (v. 11). He said this because he had come to earth to seek and to save the lost, people like the young woman and like us. Jesus had not come to condemn sinners but to live the perfect life that we should have lived and then to be condemned in our place. It is his perfect righteousness given to us that enables Jesus to say to us, "Neither do I condemn you."

If you have not yet placed your trust in Jesus, see the burning love that God has shown you in him and come to bow your knees before him. Why would you continue to close your heart to someone who has loved you with such burning passion? If you are a Christian, God says to you, "There is no condemnation for you who are in Christ Jesus. Go and sin no more." It is not that your sexual sin doesn't matter or didn't count. On the contrary, it mattered enough that Jesus had to die for it. But having counted it against Jesus, God will no longer count it against you. The guilt and shame of your sin is gone, finished, nailed to the cross, done away with forever.

This is the truth that encourages us to go and sin no more. It will be a lifelong struggle to pursue obedience in our sexuality, one in which we will often fail. In those times, we need to come back again to the cross, to remind ourselves of God's unshakable, burning love for us. We are all repeat offenders who are in desperate need of his grace. But as we behold God's incomparable love for us—the legal, affectionate, and passionate bond that, in Christ, he has entered into with his creatures—we find the love that we so crave. His grace is sufficient even for us, and it will remain sufficient until he takes us to be with him in heaven.

8

Intimacy Lost and Regained

Song of Songs 5:2—6:3

Woman
2 I slept, but my heart was awake.
The sound of my beloved, pounding on the door!

Man
"Open for me, my sister, my darling, my dove, my perfect one.
My head is filled with dew,
my locks with the drops of the night."

Woman
3 "I have stripped off my robe.
Must I put it back on again?
I have washed my feet; must I dirty them?"
4 My beloved sent his hand through the hole [in the door],
and my insides were in turmoil over him.
5 I got myself out of bed to open to my beloved:
my hands were dripping with myrrh,
and myrrh was flowing from my fingers to the handles of the bolt.
6 I myself opened to my beloved,
but my beloved had turned and gone away;
I almost died at his departure.
I sought him but did not find him;

I called him but he did not answer me.
7 The guards who go around the city found me.
They struck me and they bruised me.
The guardians of the walls took my mantle from me.
8 I charge you, daughters of Jerusalem,
if you find my beloved, what should you tell him?
That I am sick with love!

Daughters of Jerusalem
9 What makes your beloved better than other beloveds,
most beautiful of women?
What makes your beloved better than other beloveds,
that you would charge us like this?

Woman
10 My beloved is radiant and ruddy,
standing out from the crowd.
11 His head is pure gold;
his locks are like clusters of date-flowers, black like the raven.
12 His eyes are like doves
beside deep currents of water,
washed in milk,
sitting beside full [pools].
13 His cheeks are like a flowerbed of balsam,
raised beds of spices;
his lips are lilies,
dripping with liquid myrrh.
14 His arms are rods of gold,
set with jasper;
his belly is a plate of ivory,
overlaid with lapis lazuli.
15 His legs are columns of alabaster,
set on pedestals of pure gold;
his appearance is like Lebanon,
choice as cedars.
16 His palate is sweet
and all of him is desirable:
this is my beloved, this is my darling,
daughters of Jerusalem.

Daughters of Jerusalem
6:1 Where has your beloved gone,
most beautiful among women?
Where has your beloved turned,
that we may seek him with you?

Woman
2 My beloved has gone down to his garden,
to flowerbeds of balsam,
to graze in the gardens
and to gather lilies.
3 I am my beloved's and my beloved is mine
—he who grazes in the lilies.

"And so they lived happily ever after . . ." is the typical fairy-tale ending. Except that they didn't. No one ever does. Had it been a true story, Prince Charming would soon have discovered that Snow White herself could sometimes be grumpy, sleepy, and dopey, not just happy! Sleeping Beauty would sometimes have responded to true love's kiss with "Not tonight, dear; I'm tired." And as for the Beast . . . well, let's just say that perhaps Beauty should have invested some time in a little more premarital counseling. There is a man with serious anger issues that are likely to resurface in moments of stress.

None of that means that they shouldn't have had their storybook wedding, of course. If you are searching for a sinless spouse, then, like Cinderella's Prince with his glass slipper, you are likely to spend your life roaming fruitlessly throughout the land. There are no perfect people to marry—only deeply flawed sinners who will sometimes disappoint you, hurt you, and let you down. What is more, we, too, are deeply flawed sinners who will fail and disappoint our spouses in a thousand different ways. That is what this portion of the Song of Songs is about: the glorious intimacy that the lovers entered through marriage is threatened and lost for a time, before finally being restored after a lengthy search.

Our own relationships are similar. Entering marriage is not the end of your search for a spouse. It is the beginning of a lifelong pursuit, as you continually sin against each other, and then ask for forgiveness, pushing through the obstacles that threaten to divide you in search of true intimacy. The same is also true, of course, of your relationship with God through Christ, to which human marriage provides a God-given analogy. You cannot simply enter a relationship with Christ by praying a prayer or throwing a stick into the fire and then checking it off your "to do" list. You are called to a lifelong pursuit of Christ, as you continually sin against him, and then reach out afresh in repentance, pressing onward in search of true intimacy with God. Yet you should also be encouraged in your pursuit by God's prior and unfailing commitment in Christ to pursue you, even when you are running as fast as you can in the opposite direction.

Not Tonight, Dear

The poem begins with the woman half-awake and half-asleep (Song 5:2). As we commented earlier, the heart is the organ of thought in Hebrew, so when she says that she slept but her heart was awake, she means that even though she was sleeping (or falling asleep?), she was not entirely unconscious. Some commentators have assumed that she was then roused from her sleep by her beloved's actual knock on the door and that what follows is an entirely realistic description of subsequent events that night.[1] This seems unlikely, since the whole sequence has a dreamlike quality. The opening may seem straightforward enough. The man would not be the only husband in history to be locked out of his bedroom by his wife. But why did he leave so swiftly? Where did he go? Why, when she ran after him, did the city guards beat her and take her mantle? After all, her meeting with the watchmen at night in chapter 3 seemed so unthreatening. And after the encounter, presumably now in a bruised and bloodied state, why did she turn so calmly to address the daughters of Jerusalem, as if nothing had happened? These kinds of unexplained situations, bizarre events, and sudden shifts in the action are typical of dreams but not of everyday life. This is a poetic dream, not an account of actual events.

Reinforcing that view, we should note that what the woman heard at the beginning of the poem was exactly the same thing that she heard back in Song 2:8: "the sound of my beloved" (Song 5:2). This time, though, instead of bounding over the hills to come to her, the man is knocking on her door.

1. For example, Richard Brooks, *Song of Songs* (Fearn, UK: Christian Focus, 1999), 121–28; Craig Glickman, *Solomon's Song of Love: Let a Song of Songs Inspire Your Own Love Story* (Brentwood, TN: Howard, 2004), 94–99.

On both occasions, he is on the outside while she is within, and he desires them to be together. Both times, he addresses her sweetly—in this case, combining several of his favorite terms of endearment for her: "my sister, my darling, my dove, my perfect one" (v. 2). And both times, she refuses him.

Yet the similarities between the passages heighten the contrasts. In chapter 2, the man desired her to come outside with him to the open country; now he desires to come inside to be with her. Now that they are married, they don't need to find somewhere to hide: they have a marriage bed. It is clear that sexual intimacy, the same sexual intimacy that they enjoyed for the first time in the previous passage, is precisely what is on his mind. Commentators have noted a number of potential Hebrew euphemisms in the conversation that follows,[2] but you don't need to be a skilled Hebraist to catch the general drift of the conversation. He wants to make love to her, a desire that is now entirely appropriate given their married state. Yet she once again says, "No."

Whereas in chapter 2 her reasons for refusing him were wise—she was aware of the many dangers that surround premarital sex, the "little foxes" that threatened the future produce of their vineyards—here in chapter 5, her reasons are absolutely the flimsiest possible. "I have stripped off my robe. Must I put it back on again? I have washed my feet; must I dirty them?" (Song 5:3). Really? This doesn't even rise to the level of "Not tonight, dear, I have a headache." Is this the same woman who in chapter 1 was willing to brave the midday sun and the scorn of the shepherd boys just to be with her lover? Is this the girl who was fainting with love in chapter 2? Is this the woman who summoned the wide winds to blow on the oasis of her love in the previous chapter? Now it seems that she is quite content to leave him outside in the cold and rain rather than make the slightest effort to get out of her comfortable bed. As one writer has pointed out, "The tragic opposite of burning love is not necessarily fierce hate: it can be a simple bored indifference to the desires and needs of the loved one."[3]

There is presumably a reason for this coldness and indifference on her part, though the poet doesn't record the details. We don't hear of a knockdown, drag-out fight in which she throws a plate at his head, then slams the door in his face, and then bursts into tears. But there is something going on here, something to which she seems perhaps to be responding in a passive-

2. Some of these supposed euphemisms, however, may be more in the minds of the commentators than intended by the author.

3. Glickman, *Solomon's Song of Love*, 93–94.

aggressive way, rather than its simply being a matter of laziness or apathy. Instead of seeing sex as a beautiful gift that she can give to serve her spouse, the woman seems to be using it as a weapon against him, a way of punishing him.

Even then, the man makes a final attempt to bridge the gap from his side by reaching an arm through the peephole in the door (Song 5:4). It was an attempt that was always likely to fail given any reasonably designed locking system, but he at least made the effort to reach out to her, in spite of her coldness. For her part, she is once again a locked garden, as she was in chapter 4. But now, that is no longer a positive assessment of her situation. Perhaps she simply wanted to make him beg for a while.

A Change of Heart

Suddenly, something changed the woman's mind. For whatever reason, the sight and sounds of the man's efforts to reach her finally had an impact on her. Her insides were in turmoil (Song 5:4), a phrase that could simply mean that her emotions were aroused or that she was responding with sexual desire. She finally went to open the door to him, her fingers dripping with liquid myrrh—an image of sexual desire—now ready to welcome him to her bed and her body (v. 5). But alas, it is now too late. By the time the woman completed the slow-motion action of getting out of bed and fumbling with the bolt, her beloved had turned and gone, unwilling to play her games.

Now the woman is distraught and racked with fear. In Hebrew, she says literally, "My soul went out" (Song 5:6), as though her very life essence had left the building in pursuit of him. We might say, "I was devastated" or "I almost died." Having failed to respond to the man's initiative earlier, now the woman undertakes three fruitless actions ("I opened . . . I sought . . . I called," v. 6), which are a mirror image of the man's earlier efforts (he called, he sought to unbolt the door, but she did not open, vv. 2–4). The couple's desires end up moving in the same direction, but they are not synchronized, as is often the case in marriage.

The Dangerous Search for Intimacy

At this point, we return to the theme of the night search from chapter 3. Again, it is worth noticing the differences as well as the similarities. In this chapter, the necessity for the search has been created by her own slowness to respond, not merely by her beloved's absence. This time, when she was found by the watchmen as they went about the city, they immediately struck her and bruised her, taking away her mantle (Song 5:7). Presumably, they took her to be a prostitute, especially if her "mantle" is to be understood as a light and flimsy garment rather than a proper covering. The irony is profound: the one who did not want to get dressed to meet her beloved in verse 3 now has her flimsy covering stripped away by strangers. The watchmen of the walls, part of whose job it was to guard against illicit sexual encounters,[4] punished her for her unwillingness to pursue a lawful sexual encounter with her own husband.

Again, we need to remember that this is a poetic dream, not a real event. She wasn't actually beaten by the town's finest, any more than she was actually running through the town center in the dark, clad only in her nightie. Yet in the dream, her encounters with the wider community in the form of the watchmen of the walls and the daughters of Jerusalem are significant. The watchmen of the walls represent the disapproving voice of the law, whether in the shape of the wider community or her own conscience. They neither speak nor are spoken to. They simply launch into a punishment that might seem superficially appropriate but doesn't actually match the details of the case. Perhaps it is not ridiculous for watchmen to assume that a scantily clad woman out alone at night is a prostitute, but we know that this was not the case here. In the world of the dream, the beating is undeserved, a far more severe punishment than she merited.

The woman's encounter with the daughters of Jerusalem is much more helpful than her meeting with the watchmen (Song 5:8–9). This group of women has shifted roles as the Song progresses and the woman becomes more confident in her relationship. Initially, the daughters of Jerusalem were the urban sophisticates who seemed to pose a threatening contrast to the country heroine. Now, though, they seem to have become a peer group for her, her friends and intimates. Whereas she had previously charged the daughters of Jerusalem not to stir up love too soon, now she charges them to tell her beloved that she is sick with love. Instead of rebuking or beating her, the daughters of Jerusalem ask her questions: "What makes your beloved better than other beloveds, most beautiful of women?" (v. 9). These

4. See Othmar Keel, *The Song of Songs: A Continental Commentary* (Minneapolis: Fortress, 1994), 195.

questions gently prod her to reflect on the nature of her beloved and of their relationship and force her to face up to the heart of her fears, which is the fear of abandonment.

My Beloved Is Altogether Desirable

In response, the woman launches into a description of her man, beginning with a general statement about his appearance and then moving downward from his head to his feet. He is radiant and ruddy (Song 5:10), like King David in his youth, glowing with health. He is "distinguished among ten thousand" (v. 10 ESV), she says, using a word with military connotations. Unlike Solomon hiding behind his sixty mighty men, her man is at the forefront of the battle. His head is of gold (v. 11), a description that refers to his glowing appearance and value rather than his hair color. His hair is described as black like a raven, and wild and curly like date flowers. His eyes are like doves (v. 12) and his cheeks are scented like flowerbeds of spices (v. 13), while his lips are like lilies dripping with liquid myrrh. Moving down his anatomy, we shift from images of smell and taste to visual images of strength and beauty: his arms are rods of gold set with jasper (v. 14), his legs are pillars of alabaster in sockets of gold (v. 15), and his muscled abdomen is like a plate of ivory inlaid with lapis lazuli. She ends, as she began, with a more general statement about the beauty of her beloved. As in chapter 2, he is tall and straight like a tree, though this time she compares him to a cedar of Lebanon rather than an apple tree (v. 15). She still celebrates the sweet taste of his fruit, and so the center and the end of her description both focus on his lips (vv. 13, 16), which are the source of the kisses that she once again desires.

Strikingly, her description connects the man with her in key respects. His eyes are doves, just like hers; the same myrrh that was dripping from her hands now drips from his lips. She ends up calling him "my darling" (Song 5:16); this is the only place she uses this term for him, which is one of his favorite terms for her. It is as though when she looks at her beloved, the woman recognizes that he is the true complement of herself: their shared love makes one flesh from the two of them.[5]

5. Gianni Barbiero, *Song of Songs: A Close Reading*, trans. Michael Tait, SVT 144 (Leiden: Brill, 2011), 283.

I Am My Beloved's

At this point, the daughters of Jerusalem speak again. Once again, they offer neither wisdom nor advice. They simply ask a question, "Where has your beloved gone?" This simple question apparently unlocks all the insight that the woman needs. Though the daughters of Jerusalem offer to assist the woman in her search, she doesn't need their help anymore. She has had a "eureka!" moment. After talking to them, she now knows where her true love is to be found. She says, "He's gone down to his garden, to flowerbeds of balsam, to graze in the gardens and to gather lilies. I am my beloved's and my beloved is mine—he who grazes in the lilies" (Song 6:2–3).

The nature of that eureka moment might not seem immediately obvious to us. In fact, if we had been the daughters of Jerusalem, we might have been tempted to ask, "Which garden? What lilies? Did those guards hit you on the head? Maybe you should go to the emergency room at the Jerusalem City Hospital to get checked for a concussion." But if we connect what she is saying with the rest of the Song, it becomes much clearer. She herself is his garden. The flowerbeds of balsam are his cheeks (Song 5:13). When he described her body, the man spoke of her breasts as twin gazelles grazing among the lilies (4:5). And the phrase "My beloved is mine, and I am his—he who grazes among the lilies" comes directly from her own words in 2:16. In other words, the woman is saying, "I've been out in the streets desperately searching for my beloved as if he were lost forever, but he is not lost. We belong together, and even if we sin against each other, there is a bond between us that can never be broken. My beloved is mine and I am his."

Notice, though, that this time she actually reverses the statement from chapter 2. Instead of beginning with "My beloved is mine," this time she says, "I am my beloved's." This is significant because it was precisely the failure to remember that "I am my beloved's" that triggered this whole episode. She was reluctant to get up and open the door because she was thinking only of herself and her own desires. She was thinking, "My body is mine, and it belongs in my comfortable bed right now," forgetting that her body actually belongs to her husband, just as his belongs to her. Furthermore, it was her failure to remember that "I am my beloved's" that triggered her panicked nighttime search for him. She was terrified that because of her selfishness, she had lost him forever. But when the daughters of Jerusalem prompted her to think about who her beloved really was, she finally realized that she didn't need to be afraid of losing him. In spite of everything, it was still true that "I am my beloved's." In the poem, she hasn't actually found him, but her fears have been relieved. She had forgotten the permanence of the man's commitment to her. This, combined with his trustworthy character, meant that she could rest assured that he would always come back and be reconciled with her, even when she had sinned against him in real ways. Their bond of burning love was not so easily shattered, even when she acted in ways that were cold and callous.

I Am Mine

This poem challenges us to see all the ways that we behave in our relationships as though "my beloved is mine and I am mine as well." We constantly act as though we belong to ourselves and rule over our own little kingdoms, which others may enter, but only if they wish to bow down and serve us. Don Miller expresses it like this:

> Living in community made me realize one of my faults: I was addicted to myself. All I thought about was myself. The only thing I thought about was myself. . . . I discovered that my mind is like a radio that picks up only one station, the one that plays me: K-DON, *all Don, all the time.*[6]

If we are honest, we are all relentlessly self-absorbed. In marriage, one area where this commonly plays itself out is sex. When we are young and wrestling with intense hormonal urges, many of us face the difficult challenge of how to keep from sleeping together too soon, before we marry. We are still living in chapter 2 of the Song, and imagine that marriage will solve all our sexual struggles. But there is a chapter 5 after the wedding, a time when it is easy for sex to become a different kind of problem. In some cases, the husband is more interested in intimacy than the wife, while in others it is the reverse. In still other cases, the man simply moves much more quickly than the woman does, and they are not synchronized in their desires. What is more, difficulties in other areas of the marital relationship inevitably affect our sex lives.

6. Don Miller, *Blue like Jazz: Nonreligious Thoughts on Christian Spirituality* (Nashville: Thomas Nelson, 2003), 181 (original emphasis).

Yet the fundamental problem is almost never sex. It is self. My radio station is playing K-Me, all me, all the time, and so I become absorbed by all the ways in which you are not pleasing me as you should. I think that I should be able to have sex as often or as rarely as I wish, instead of asking how often or rarely my spouse would like to be loved in this way. This was an issue that Paul addressed in ancient Corinth, a society that was as obsessed with sex as our own. Some Christians responded to the wanton excess of their culture by going to the opposite extreme and pursuing celibacy, even within marriage. Yet Paul's counsel was neither excess nor total abstinence but rather sexual self-giving within marriage. He wrote:

> But because of the temptation to sexual immorality, each man should have his own wife and each woman her own husband. The husband should give to his wife her conjugal rights, and likewise the wife to her husband. For the wife does not have authority over her own body, but the husband does. Likewise the husband does not have authority over his own body, but the wife does. Do not deprive one another, except perhaps by agreement for a limited time, that you may devote yourselves to prayer; but then come together again, so that Satan may not tempt you because of your lack of self-control. (1 Cor. 7:2–5)

Notice Paul's reasoning. Your body is not your own in marriage: *you* are not your own. In marriage, you need to give yourself to your spouse, and one way in which that will be true is sexually. Of course, this doesn't simply mean that the wife always gets up and opens the door for her husband. It also means his being sensitive to the fact that this may not be a good time for her, or being patient enough to wait for her desire to catch up to his.

You don't have to be married to begin to practice this truth. It is not just married people who are relentlessly self-absorbed, though marriage does tend to expose our self-absorption in a particularly intense way. We are self-absorbed in all our relationships and need to learn how to die to ourselves and our own interests and put others first in every area of life. Before marriage, we are often utterly self-absorbed in our dating relationships. That is why we are so desperately insecure, so eager to get or to give that ring, defining a relationship in which we can finally say, "My beloved is mine." Often, we are not really seeking to love and serve the person we are dating, or to find out what is best for that person, whether that is a relationship with us or with someone else. We are certainly not trusting God to lead us to the best person to marry, or perhaps even to lead us safely down a path of singleness that might give us more opportunities to serve him. Often, our dating is all about us, all the time—about what we believe being in a relationship, or not being in a relationship, says about us.

Paradoxically, our insecurity and self-centeredness lead us to the worst possible approach to dating. We stay in a toxic relationship that we should leave, or we settle for someone who isn't really a good match for us, because we are terrified that if we terminate this relationship, no one else will want us. Alternatively, we bounce from relationship to relationship because no one can meet our impossibly demanding expectations. Either way, it is all about us.

Our other relationships are also often all about us. It is true of our friendships, in which we want people to listen to us and our problems endlessly but get impatient and restless if they start to place a burden on us. It is often true in our parenting, as we demand that our children measure up to our expectations for their lives. When they are small, they must not embarrass us by misbehaving or get in the way of our work or our pleasure. When they are older, they need to fulfill our dreams by pouring themselves into academics, baseball, ballet, or law school—or perhaps all of the above. It is also true of us as children. We believe that our parents exist to provide for us financially and to enable us to live the life of our dreams with minimal effort on our part. Do we ever even ask how we, as children, can serve our parents and give ourselves for their sake?

For the woman in the poem, "all me, all the time" wasn't working too well. It left her feeling alone and insecure, frantically running through the dark streets searching for someone who could not be found. Perhaps you can identify with her nighttime identity. You, too, have been scouring the dark streets of your life for meaning and hope. Perhaps the watchmen of the walls have been beating you up, as well, whether these figures represent the condemnatory words of others or the demanding voice of your own conscience. Guilt can leave you bruised and battered internally, even if on the outside there are no visible wounds. Where is true peace to be found?

Finding Peace

In the poem, the woman doesn't find true peace on her own but through the simple questions of the daughters of Jerusalem. Ironically, "all me, all the time" doesn't produce much insight even into me, let alone into my relationships. Even though the daughters of Jerusalem have no advanced degrees in counseling, they seem to know that questions are often better than comments. It is better to ask someone what the person is feeling and why than to assume that you have infinite insight into the deep wells of the human heart and can tell someone exactly what the problem is. In the poem, the simple questions that the daughters of Jerusalem ask provide comfort by reminding the woman of what she has forgotten: the beauty, strength, and character of her beloved, as well as the depth of their love relationship, which together mean that he cannot possibly be gone forever. In spite of their problems, she is still her beloved's and he is still hers. They had made a lasting commitment to each other that would endure through trying times.

Of course, that kind of reflection will not always comfort us in this way in our human relationships. Sometimes we feel abandoned and alone because we really are alone and abandoned by those who should have been there for us. Our friends and spouses may really prove to be untrustworthy and unreliable, so that there is no comfort to be found by dwelling on their character. In fact, that should be one of our goals in the dating process: to form a clear picture of this person's character, which will be revealed most clearly when we let the person down and disappoint him or her, and when that person does the same to us. Is he or she able to forgive us and encourage us in our brokenness? Is that person able to repent and respond rightly to his or her own brokenness? If you find someone of whom those things are true, you likely have a sinner that you can live with and grow with, even if his outward appearance looks absolutely nothing like the Adonis described in the poem. If you do not look for someone like that, though, the inevitable problems that arise once you are married may well drive you apart rather than bringing you back together again.

I Am His Forever

Some of us don't have spouses to comfort and encourage us through the dark nights. In some cases, the people who ought to have shepherded and loved us actually betrayed and abandoned us. Others may be single or widowed. Yet even the very best of spouses will frequently let us down and sin against us. They, too, will often expose the fact that their radio stations are playing K-Them, all the time. Our peace and rest cannot ultimately be found in any human lover. Our souls long for a better, deeper, and truer relationship than any human marriage can possibly provide. We need someone who is always utterly faithful and reliable, completely and perfectly beautiful, so that when we think about his character, we have absolutely no question about his commitment to us, someone of whom we can truly say, "My beloved is mine and I am his *forever*." We need someone who will stand at the door and continue to knock even when we are unreasonably cold and fickle. We need Jesus.

In the book of Revelation, Jesus says, "Behold, I stand at the door and knock. If anyone hears my voice and opens the door, I will come in to him and eat with him, and he with me" (Rev. 3:20). It is a familiar verse that has spawned a thousand (often tacky) artistic renditions. But did you ever notice to whom Jesus says these words? It was to the church at Laodicea, a church that was neither hot nor cold but lukewarm. The churchgoers at Laodicea said, "I am rich, I have prospered, and I need nothing" (v. 17), when in reality they were poor, blind, and naked. They were comfortably all about themselves, all the time, lost in the dark while not even realizing their own lostness. Jesus had some challenging words to say to these comfortable sinners, words of loving reproof. If they remained in their lukewarm state, he would spew them out of his mouth. Jesus told them that they needed to repent of their self-centeredness and find their sufficiency in him alone.

Yet it was precisely to these lost, blind, and self-centered people that Jesus proclaimed that in spite of their lukewarmness, he still stood knocking on their door. He had not gone away and left them as they deserved. He had not abandoned them to their comfortable blindness and self-centeredness. Even then, Jesus stood at the door, not with a staff in his hands like the watchmen of the walls, ready to beat and bruise them for their sin. Instead, he stood there patiently offering them the salve that their blind eyes so desperately needed, ready to clothe their nakedness with his glorious garments, ready to come into their house, not so that he could scold and nag and upbraid, but so that he could show his unchanging love and care for them by sharing a fellowship meal together.

This is the Husband on whose commitment we all need to reflect daily. Jesus is so patient with us—the absolute opposite of someone who is all about himself. The irony is that this world really is all about him, since he created it.

The radio stations of this world should be tuned to K-God—all to the glory of God, all the time. Yet Jesus set aside his own glory for the sake of his bride. The Extraordinary One made himself ordinary, as a humble carpenter in a backwater Galilee town. The Beautiful One took up a form with no beauty, and even what beauty he had was then disfigured horribly on the cross. He came not to be served by others but to serve and give his life as a ransom. This is the God who in Jesus still stands at the door and knocks, calling lost and frightened sinners into a close and intimate fellowship with him.

Have you ever opened the door of your heart to Jesus? We are not born with hearts that are open to God. Instead, we are born like the Laodiceans: cold toward God, or indifferent, which is simply its own form of idolatry. We are all about ourselves. But God gently (and sometimes not so gently) breaks in. He opens blind eyes, softens hard hearts, and raises dead souls. He gives us the desire and the ability to open the door of our hearts, and then he calls us to open to him. Are you hearing that call, perhaps for the first time? Open! He will come in, no matter how dirty and messy your heart is! Repent of your self-centeredness and self-worship and come to bow at his feet. Receive the truest love that you will ever find in the entire universe: God's love for you in Jesus.

Christian, as you search your own heart, what do you find toward Christ? If you are like me, you will often find coldness and indifference. He has inscribed letters of burning love to you in his Word, but you can't be bothered to pick up your Bible and read it, or if you do, you soon wish you were surfing the Internet instead. He invites you to meet him for fellowship in church, through songs and preaching and eating together at the Lord's Supper, yet your mind flits here and there, wondering what's for lunch or what that person in the next row really thinks of you. What is Jesus to do with us? We deserve to be spat out of his mouth, divorced for our long history of spiritual adultery.

Maybe at this moment the enormity of your sins is pressing in upon you and you are terrified that Jesus will give up on you. You feel lost in the dark streets of Jerusalem, searching but not finding. You read your Bible, but you don't find Jesus there. You try to pray, but it seems as though your prayers bounce off the ceiling. Perhaps you no longer have the warm experiences of God that you used to have as a younger Christian, and you are puzzled by your own lukewarmness.

Visit with the daughters of Jerusalem, and let their questions counsel you. Go back and reflect again on the wonderful reality of your true Beloved. Though you are weak and fickle, Jesus is altogether beautiful and glorious. Not only is he faithful to you, but as a human being he has also been faithful to God in your place. When he read the Scriptures, his heart always delighted in the wisdom of his Father's Word. When he went to the synagogue, his mind never wandered or rested on his own interests. He came to do his Father's will, even when it was most painful for him. Jesus was faithful even when it truly meant being abandoned by God. He was literally bruised and beaten to a pulp by those who ought to have been the watchmen over Israel, left in the complete darkness of the cross, scanning the skies for his beloved Father's face but seeing nothing in return. Yet in the midst of all that darkness, Jesus never doubted that he was still his Father's and his Father was his. With his final breath on earth, Jesus commended his spirit into his Father's faithful care (Luke 23:46).

We fear. We doubt. We sin. We wander in the darkness. But Jesus Christ trusted, believed, obeyed, and followed faithfully for us. And so in the midst of our often-failing struggles to love those around us faithfully, when our hearts flare up in anger and our self-centeredness is on full display, we may return and rest in him, finding fresh assurance as we meditate on his beauty and faithfulness. When the Lord finally gives you the grace to get out of bed, cross the floor, and open the door, you will find that your Beloved is still there, saying to you, "I am my beloved's and my beloved is mine, both now and forever."

9

Making Up Is Hard to Do

Song of Songs 6:1–12

Daughters of Jerusalem
6:1 Where has your beloved gone,
most beautiful among women?
Where has your beloved turned,
that we may seek him with you?

Woman
2 My beloved has gone down to his garden,
to flowerbeds of balsam,
to graze in the gardens
and to gather lilies.
3 I am my beloved's and my beloved is mine
—he who grazes in the lilies.

Man
4 You are beautiful, my darling, like Tirzah;
lovely like Jerusalem;
awe-inspiring like [armies] with banners.
5 Turn your eyes away from me,
for they disturb me!
Your hair is like a flock of goats
streaming down from Mount Gilead.

[6] Your teeth are like a flock of ewe-lambs
which are going up from the washing,
all of them bearing twins
—none of them bereaved.
[7] Your cheek is a slice of pomegranate
behind your veil.
[8] There are sixty queens, eighty concubines
and virgins without number.
[9] But she is unique, my dove, my perfect one;
she is unique to her mother,
pure to the one who bore her.
Daughters saw her and called her blessed;
queens and concubines envied her and praised her.
[10] Who is this that looks down like the dawn,
beautiful like the full moon,
incomparable like the sun's heat,
awe-inspiring like [the heavenly armies] with banners?

Woman
[11] I went down to a garden of walnut trees,
to look at the shoots of the valley,
to see if the vine had budded
and the pomegranates were in bloom.
[12] I don't know what's up with me.
You set me in chariots with a nobleman.

What makes a marriage last? In a divorce-saturated culture, why do some people stay together when others split apart? Some might say "compatibility." Some people are just naturally easier to live with, while others are high-maintenance. It is certainly true that while everyone enters marriage with significant baggage, some people have more obvious challenges to face than others. Yet even seemingly compliant spouses can be as hard to endure as the yelling and screaming variety. Sooner or later, no matter how "compatible" you are, significant differences emerge in any marriage that will threaten to bring about a rift between you. If you don't have any means of resolving those differences, your marriage is headed for trouble. Indeed, sometimes marriages that start out with many disagreements end up stronger for it, because the husband and wife learned early on how to settle those differences. That is not always the case, by any means, but profound differences don't have to doom a relationship.

As we saw in the previous chapter, our married couple hit a significant bump in the road in the dream sequence of Song 5:3–6:3. The man came home late one night in a romantic mood, but the woman wasn't interested. By the time she changed her mind and got out of bed to open the door for him, he was gone. The woman went out looking for him through the streets of the city and got a sound beating from the city watchmen for her troubles. She ended up talking to her girlfriends, the daughters of Jerusalem, whose simple questions got her back on track. They asked her about her beloved, and as she recalled his beauty and stability, she finally realized that he wouldn't abandon her. He was still committed to her, as she was to him. She affirmed hopefully that she would find him in the same place that he always was, in his garden—the garden of their love, grazing among the lilies.

In the Garden of Delights

The present passage ends with the woman[1] recounting how she followed the man down to that garden, which is now described as a garden of nut trees (Song 6:11). Fruitful trees regularly symbolize the couple's enjoyment of their love, whether apple trees, vines, or date palms. She went there to see whether the vines had budded and the pomegranates were in bloom. This is exactly the language that the man used in 2:12–13 to describe the springtime blooming of romance, the evidence that it was time for love. In chapter 2, it wasn't yet time, in spite of the man's protestations. In chapter 4, after their wedding, the harvest season finally arrived when they could pluck the delightful ripe fruit of their love. But now the woman found herself in doubt again. Was she really right in her earlier confident proclamation that her lover was hers and she was his? When she got to the garden, would the woman actually find that their love was still in bloom, or would she discover that a cold winter frost had settled over their relationship because of her snub, killing the tender blossoms?

1. Some people think that the man is still speaking at this point, but I think that the words make more sense coming from the woman. Certainly, the enigmatic verse 12 seems to fit the woman better than the man. See J. Cheryl Exum, *Song of Songs: A Commentary*, OTL (Louisville, KY: Westminster John Knox, 2005), 223.

So what happened when she arrived at the garden? Unfortunately, Song 6:12 is one of the most challenging verses in the Bible to translate. Commentators spend many pages justifying their particular interpretations of a series of words that literally say, "I don't know—my soul—it (or you) set me—chariots of Amminadab" (or "my noble people" or "with a noble"). My translation is: "I don't know what's up with me. You set me in chariots with a nobleman." Most agree that the woman's words display a state of emotional turmoil[2]—a turmoil that ended in a state of exultation, like that of riding along in an exalted vehicle. We might paraphrase it like this: "I was blown away, swept off my feet, and carried up into the clouds with Prince Charming." What caused this transformation from the cautious but fearful optimism with which the woman entered the garden, hoping to find some buds of their love left intact, to such expressions of rapturous delight? It was the words that the man said to her, which are recorded in verses 4–10. In other words, the man's response to their conflict blew her away.

You Are Still Beautiful, My Darling

What was it in the man's response that had this enormous impact on the woman? To begin with, the man responded immediately, affirming the stability of his love for her. The most obvious feature of this speech is the exact repetition of a number of lines from the man's earlier poem of praise in chapter 4. Some things have not changed in his attitude to her, and will never change. He starts out with the same summary statement: "You are beautiful, my darling" (Song 6:4; see 4:1). *Darling* is not merely a general term of endearment but a word that speaks of friendship and companionship. It is one of the man's favorite terms for the woman. He goes on to repeat himself in other ways, with only minor variations. Her hair is still like a lively flock of black goats, streaming down Mount Gilead; her teeth are still like a flock of lambs coming up from the washing, each with its perfectly white matching partner; her cheek is still like a blushing slice of pomegranate behind her veil (6:5–7; see 4:1–3).

Why all this repetition? A poet as creative as the writer of the Song of Songs is not merely running out of new things to say and therefore cutting

2. The Hebrew phrase "I don't know my own soul" means something like this: "I can't figure out what's going on with me." For a fuller discussion, see Iain M. Duguid, *The Song of Songs: An Introduction and Commentary*, TOTC 19 (Downers Grove, IL: InterVarsity Press, 2015), 140–41.

and pasting in some tired old lines from a previous poem. No, what is significant here is *precisely* what the man says and what he omits. Omitted from the previous poem are the references to her lips and to her body below her face—her neck and breasts. Given the fact that their fight was over sex, the last thing the man wants to do is to give the impression that he just wants to make up so that he can get back into bed with her. So he passes over the more erotic elements of his description. At the same time, the repetition of the other elements of his former description stresses the fact that he hasn't changed in his fundamental view of her attractiveness. He found her lovely before, and he still does, in spite of their quarrel. As Shakespeare put it so beautifully, "Love is not love that alters when it alteration finds."[3] He doesn't respond to her coldness with angry words or with a lasting frosty coldness of his own. He did walk away from the closed door for a time. That was probably wise, giving her space rather than seeking to force the issue. But as soon as she appears in front of him, the man's words are not words of anger or reproach but of love.

Particularly interesting is the reference to the veil, which carries over from chapter 4. As we said earlier, women were not generally veiled in public in Israel; in the poetic dream she left the house wearing very little and was stripped of even that light clothing along the way (Song 5:7). So it is doubtful that she would have been wearing a veil at this point. But veils often had a connection with the marriage ceremony in the ancient Near East, so the reference to her "cheek . . . behind [her] veil" (6:7) is a way of saying, "You are as lovely as you were on the day I married you. Remember that day? I said 'Forever—till death do us part,' and I meant it. My love for you has not changed, and it will not change."

You Are Awesome

Some things have changed in their relationship, though. The man doesn't simply repeat the poem verbatim from their wedding day. Their relationship has grown through their experience of conflict, and it has new depths and complexities that weren't there before. We can see this in the comparison of her beauty to the cities of Tirzah and Jerusalem. These were both capital

3. William Shakespeare, "Sonnet 116," in *The Oxford Shakespeare: Complete Sonnets and Poems* (Oxford: Oxford University Press, 2008), 613.

cities: Tirzah was the original capital of the northern kingdom, before Omri moved it to Samaria, while Jerusalem was the capital of the south. Naming these particular cities in the same breath means linking two things that belonged together, but had at times existed as separated rivals.

But this is not quite like nicknaming your bride *Pittsburgh*, *Hoboken*, or even *Los Angeles*. Both of these biblical cities had names that were filled with meaning: *Tirzah* means "desirable, pleasant," and *Jerusalem* "City of Peace." While it is common in the Bible to compare cities to beautiful women, it is quite unusual to compare women to beautiful cities. Ancient cities had walls and were defended, keeping their allies safe within and their enemies safely out. The idea of the woman as a defensible location was hinted at in the earlier poem, where her neck was likened to the tower of David, decorated with warrior's shields (Song 4:4). Yet on that occasion, the shields were hung up peacefully, and the man was welcomed into the city that he had conquered through love. Here, however, the image of the woman as a beautiful city leads him to describe her as *Awesome*, in the literal sense that she evokes his awe. As the French would say, she is "*Formidable!*"[4] The same Hebrew word is used elsewhere to describe the terrifying effect of seeing the Babylonian army (Hab. 1:7), and here, too, she is described as "bannered," which presumably refers to the standards of an army drawn up in battle array. Instead of "He brought me to the house of wine, and his banner over me was love" (Song 2:4), this suggests something more like this: "She closed her gates against me and mustered the banners of her army behind high walls."

The same awesome and terrible power features in the man's description of her eyes. Perhaps no part of the anatomy is as revealing of the soul as the eyes. In chapter 4 the man described her eyes as beautiful doves, as harmless and gentle as it is possible for an animal to be. Now, however, her eyes disturb and confuse him. The verb is used elsewhere to mean "to make someone tremble." The comparable verb used in the Greek translation can describe a bird's feathers standing on end. "Your gaze drives me crazy," we might say. Yet while he finds it hard to endure her gaze, the man still can't take his eyes off her. She fascinates and unsettles him at the same time in equal measure. He can't live without her and can hardly live with her. He is in awe of her complexity and brilliance, dazzled by the challenge of being in a deep and profound relationship with this complicated human being.

4. Ellen F. Davis, *Proverbs, Ecclesiastes, and the Song of Songs*, Westminster Bible Companion (Louisville, KY: Westminster John Knox, 2000), 286.

You Are Unique

The third aspect of the man's speech is the declaration of her uniqueness. When things get difficult in their relationship, he cannot simply trade her in for another version of the same, for there is no other version of the same. This is something that someone like Solomon, with all his sexual partners, would never be able to understand. Sixty wives and eighty concubines (Song 6:8) takes the normal Hebrew poetic pairing of "three . . . and four" and ramps it up twentyfold, so that we end up with twenty times seven in total. One hundred forty women is a poetically complete set of wives and concubines, literally a "full house"—though it is a mere fraction of the historical Solomon's actual seven hundred wives and three hundred concubines (see 1 Kings 11:3).

Some men might think that it would be rather enjoyable to own such a collection of women. Yet anyone who has so many wives and concubines, together with unnumbered young women ready to take their place if any one of them should drop out, will never build the kind of relationship that this man and woman have. If one woman has a closed door, he can simply move on to the next. There is no need ever to reach out across the barriers that form in real relationships, no need to apologize and then kiss and make up for hurts inflicted or suffered. Quantity of women is not only not the same thing as quality of relationships; it is exactly the opposite.

The man in the poem, however, has chosen a different path. He has chosen the way of utterly committed, lifelong monogamy—a whole life devoted to one single person. She is unique, his dove, his perfect one (Song 6:9). For a moment, the walls have come down, the armies have laid down their weapons, and she is once again his dove, as she was in chapter 4. Her sins and her flaws are not remembered against her and continually dredged up again. She is perfect in his eyes.

Nor is the man alone in this opinion: she is equally unique and pure to her mother as well. Even if there are sisters who share her genetic makeup and upbringing, there are none to match her beauty and character. The other daughters rise up and bless her, while the queens and the royal concubines—those who feature daily in the court gossip columns for their clothes, wealth, and luxuries—envy her because she has what none of them can ever have, in spite of their affluence: the unique commitment of one man. The women to whom she feared she could never match up in chapter 1 are precisely those who now wish that they were her. If the language of Song 6:9 sounds familiar, it is because it is borrowed from Proverbs 31:28, the description of the ideal wife. Here in the Song of Songs, the daughters and the other women take the place of the children and the husband in the poem from Proverbs by praising her unique attributes and envying her blessedness.

The content of their praise, as the man recounts it, reiterates the same attributes with which the man's speech began. The woman is compared to the dawn, the moon, and the sun (Song 6:10), each of which was often viewed as a deity in the ancient Near East. In other words, the court women are in total awe of her presence, for she seems exalted to the heavens, gazing down like the dawn. She is as bright and pale as the full moon, not dark like the curtains of Kedar (1:5). Her gaze is as burning as the noonday sun, the power that she feared had burned her into unattractiveness in 1:6. She seems almost like a divine being to those around her, so awesome is her appearing.

These words of praise, awe, and affirmation on the lips of her lover have an emotional impact on the woman. She went down to the nut garden, hoping perhaps to find a few blossoms that had survived the frost of her coldness. What she discovered when she got there was awe and wonder, a friendship that was still on fire, a love that was still burning with white-hot intensity. No wonder she was confused and overwhelmed, blown away by such unexpected and gracious words. No wonder she felt that she had been caught up into the clouds in ecstasy, like an undeserving commoner picked out from the crowd to ride through town in a royal chariot.

The Positive Power of Conflict

This poem speaks profound truth about our own relationships. To begin with, we can see that the conflict between the man and the woman actually led to a deepening and strengthening of their relationship. A healthy relationship is not one in which no conflict ever occurs, but one in which that conflict gets resolved. The only way to have a relationship in which there is no conflict is to marry someone who just doesn't care. In that case, though, there will be no deep merging of your souls. If you truly care about someone, he or she will have the power to hurt you deeply, both because you want what is best for that person and because what he or she thinks of you really matters.

So it is not generally a good sign if you get engaged to someone with whom you have never had a fight. You may both be wonderfully compatible, even-tempered people, or one or both of you may be terminally avoiding conflict. I speak with knowledge, as a charter member of "Conflict-Avoiders Anonymous." I hate conflict and run from its appearance. In my own marriage, I tend to be compliant and easy to get along with, but the result is that my wife, Barb, is never really sure whether I like something or am just too nervous to speak up. As a result, little issues that could easily be resolved become big issues, and big issues tend to spiral out of control until finally one of us forces the other actually to face up to the problem. Sooner or later, if you truly love someone, he or she is going to annoy you intensely, and it is neither wise nor healthy to conceal and bury those hurts and disappointments as if nothing had happened.

Of course, it is not the conflict itself that deepens the relationship. Some couples bicker and fight constantly in all kinds of toxic ways, to the point at which it is almost a relief to everyone who knows them when they break up. When we fight, we can and do inflict real and deep wounds on those we love. But in a healthy relationship, those wounds get bandaged and healed. The conflict gets resolved, and the couple moves forward with a deeper and stronger bond than they had before.

What is more, this poem gives us a model for what conflict resolution looks like. The man doesn't hold a grudge over the way in which the woman hurt him. He doesn't dredge up the seventeen previous times she has done the same thing and ask the judge for those counts also to be taken into consideration against her. Although she left him outside a closed door, he provides an open door for her to come back, without groveling. Upon her return, she finds unchanging love and affirmation, not condemnation and retribution. The man recites all the ways in which she is still beautiful in his eyes, while tactfully avoiding the immediate subject of the fight. He affirms his deep respect for and need of her, as well as his lifelong commitment to her as a unique individual. He makes no threats or accusations; rather, he celebrates her singularity. She is his one and only, his amazingly awesome one. No wonder she melts and is overwhelmed when she hears his words!

Have you ever been in the woman's situation here? You have sinned against someone you love intensely and know that you deserve to receive coldness, anger, and harshness from him or her. Yet instead, what you actually received was love, acceptance, and warm forgiveness. What an amazing and joyful experience that is!

Unique, Permanent Commitment

Increasingly, such a unique lifelong commitment between one man and one woman is rare in our society. We may not know anyone who has sixty wives and eighty concubines (though if there were such a person, he would probably be given his own reality television show). Yet in our culture, we certainly have plenty of relationships that lack a unique, lifelong commitment. In fact, it almost seems that we train our children to adopt that perspective toward relationships by encouraging them to date a series of people casually in their teenage years, with absolutely no intention or likelihood that this relationship will ever end in marriage. Far from preparing young people for a single relationship in which they give themselves completely and permanently to one person, this approach seems more likely to train them to have one eye on the exit door at all times. If things don't work out in this relationship (by which we mean that "if this person isn't pleasing me right now"), we can just move on to the next one. And the next one after that. Perhaps it is little wonder that we bring the same attitude into our marriages, which become equally fragile.

We are encouraged by society to do the same thing with our sexuality. Instead of regarding sex as a unique gift that is to be guarded until marriage, our culture views it as normal and healthy to engage sexually with a series of partners before marriage—our premarital concubines, so to speak. Yet if marriage is intended to be unique and lifelong—a giving of yourself completely and absolutely to the one person who is the sun and the moon to you—it makes sense to wait until marriage before engaging in sex, no matter what your hormones are telling you.

Being sinners, we can get this wrong in many different ways. Some have failed by sleeping with one or more members of the opposite sex before marriage. Others have simply defined what they are doing as "not really sex," just "friends with benefits." Perhaps we stay away from sex but have engaged in emotionally committed relationships in which we pull away and hurt people whenever it looks like the friendship might be getting serious. Or we go to the opposite extreme and insist on a legally binding marriage proposal before we are willing to share a cup of coffee alone with a member of the opposite sex. Perhaps we even swear off relationships altogether, because we don't want to risk the pain and the hurt that inevitably come with them.

In contrast to all these perversions, the Song holds out a beautiful vision of marriage as it was meant to be: one man and one woman who have a deep and awe-inspiring union that is profound enough to withstand the struggles and strains that come along when two sinners live together. They have a bond of forgiveness and love forged out of the uniqueness of their commitment to each other on their wedding day, a dazzling love that will not let the other person go, even when they are driving each other absolutely crazy.

The Primacy of Marriage

Perhaps it also seems countercultural in our context that there is no Song of Songs about the beauty of graduate school or career advancement. Many people today feel pressured to put the search for a lifelong spouse behind preparation for a fulfilling and rewarding career. We think that we will address marriage later, once we have the other parts of our lives in place. Yet while the Bible certainly calls us to work hard and serve others with our gifts, it doesn't celebrate work in the same way that it celebrates the beauty of marriage. We are called to work to support ourselves and our families, and it is a beautiful gift of God if we can find joy and satisfaction in that work, but work was never intended to be a substitute for deep and strong relationships. Shouldn't the pursuit of relationships therefore have a higher priority than work in our thinking about our lives?

Of course, not everyone is called to be married. Single people are still called to deep and strong relationships in which they experience and give forgiveness and restitution, however. The church should be a place where single people and families mingle together in precisely such deep and rich webs of relationship. A mark of the depth of these relationships is the fact that when we offend one another, we care enough to pursue healing for those hurts. In order to achieve that depth of relationship, we may sometimes need to put the pursuit of those relationships ahead of the pursuit of career advancement and personal comfort and fulfillment. Single people can easily feel that they are free of any ties, when in reality they need to work even harder than married people to develop deep and lasting relationships. They may need to think twice about a career move to a new city, which would mean severing their connections with their church family and starting over from scratch in a new church. Meanwhile, churches need to think seriously about how to foster relationships in which singles and families become bonded together in a lasting way.

Conflict with God

None of us has such a perfect relationship with another human being. At best, we have a pale approximation of the true love that will not let us go, the best of all loves, the love of God for his people. Most of us fall very far short indeed, daily failing to pursue or to demonstrate the forgiveness to which the gospel calls us. We may be struggling and failing to forgive a spouse or family member who has failed us or sinned against us in a deep and painful way. Far from receiving the person back with open arms, we stand with pursed lips and an angry scowl. We know that we should forgive, but we won't. Oh, how we all need to be touched more deeply by the good news of the gospel!

How does this poem, as one stanza in the best of all songs, illuminate our relationship with Christ? To begin with, the importance of conflict for relational growth explains one of the greatest tensions in our Christian lives, which is this: we want our relationship with God to be smooth and easy, while God designed it to be real and deep. Why does God make our lives so difficult, when he has the power to make them so straightforward? Why does he bring so many problems and challenges into our pursuit of jobs, relationships, and health? Why do we struggle with repeated failures in our relationships, or a deep and abiding loneliness in our hearts, or a continual struggle with besetting sin? Why does it sometimes seem that God turns away and leaves us alone in the middle of our pain? Why is he so frustratingly and maddeningly unwilling to fix our problems?

There are lots of possible answers to those questions, but one of them is that God is deeply committed to building our relationship with him into something that has depth, substance, and maturity—qualities that relationships can acquire only through many challenges. It is only through difficulties that we learn to give up our natural independence and lean on him, and that trusting God's wisdom, love, and goodness becomes a lived reality rather than a theoretical concept. It is through our repeated sin that we learn the magnitude of his grace and through our repeated fearfulness and unfaithfulness that we see the true beauty of his faithful love.

Appreciating the Differences

This relational depth and complexity is one of the reasons why God chose to image his relationship with us through the picture of marriage between a man and a woman, a joining not just of two different people, but of two different sexes, with all our hardwired diversity that almost guarantees frustration and conflict. Men and women are not the same, and marriage forces us to confront the "otherness" of the opposite sex. One of the sanctifying aspects of marriage is thus the daily opportunity to die to ourselves and our way of doing things, along with growing in the richness that comes from seeing a different perspective on life. As a woman, Barb doesn't see things the way I do. Often, with Professor Henry Higgins in *My Fair Lady*, I wish that she would see how obviously right my "manly" perspective is! Yet as I grow in maturity and wisdom, I find that after many years of living with Barb, I can now begin to channel Barb's perspective into different situations. I can ask myself, "What would Barb do?" and explore the possibility—often the probability—that her approach would actually be better than the one that comes instinctively to me. There is a richness in the diversity of the sexes in marriage that is designed to deepen us as people.

So, too, as we walk with God, years of seeing God act in ways in which we would never act start to bear fruit. We learn that he has good purposes for bringing into our lives challenging circumstances that we would never have chosen for ourselves. We start to learn how a holy, gracious, all-wise Being speaks to fallen humans, challenging our sin yet nonetheless embracing us in forgiveness. We begin to see the costliness of his mercy and the awesome painfulness of his commitment to us and to our sanctification. Through the work of the Holy Spirit as he opens our eyes and transforms our hearts, we slowly begin to learn how to interact with others with similar holiness and grace, forgiving as we have been forgiven and loving as we have been loved, trusting that God is up to good things for us and for them, too, even when we find it difficult to understand what he is doing.

A Loving and Unchanging God

When we come to our senses and recognize our own sin, turning back to God from our repeated pursuit of our idols, perhaps we are still fearful of what we may find. We are unsure whether there will be a welcome for us after the ways in which we have sinned and let him down. Yet what we discover from our God when we return to him is nothing less than his unique and unchanging love and affirmation. We all have divided and selfish hearts that are constantly closing the door in God's face. We are often too lazy and self-centered to get out of bed and pursue a deeper relationship with him. We wander away in pursuit of our own desires and pleasure. We even use our own righteousness and successful pursuit of an obedient lifestyle as a means of avoiding having to admit our deep need of him. But when the Lord opens our eyes and changes our hearts and draws us back to meet him again, we find that he has made a unique, lifelong—eternity-long—commitment to his people. The garden of his love for us is still constantly, beautifully in full bloom.

Shouldn't that repeated experience of repentance and return change how we respond to the demands of God's holy wisdom? Her past experience would surely have an impact on the woman's heart the next time the man came knocking on the door. So, too, our repeated experience of God's open-armed forgiveness should soften our hard hearts to the difficult things that we know God is calling us to do. Perhaps we know that we should extend the same love and forgiveness to someone who has hurt us significantly, or that we should turn away from some sin that is so alluring to us, or strive for some new obedience that we have been putting off for a while. What will melt our hard hearts and draw us toward God? Is it not reflecting afresh on God's grace and mercy toward us in Christ? When we recall the surprising love and endless forgiveness that God has shown to us, then those laws and duties that once seemed harsh and unbearable are turned into joyful acts of service and love. How could Hosea have fulfilled his painful calling of loving a woman who repeatedly sullied his reputation, rejected his love, and fled from his caring embrace? It could surely only have been through long and profound reflection on the grace and mercy that the Lord had shown to Israel and to Hosea himself, as they had likewise rejected him.

When the Lord speaks to us, he stills our fears of abandonment and turns the man's hyperbolic praise of the woman into an ultimate reality within us, both as individuals and as the church. God really is transforming us into something awesome and terrible, far more glorious than we could bear to look at right now. Through our suffering, through our growing awareness of our own brokenness and need, even through our sin, God is making us into holy and gospel-loving people, who will shine like stars throughout eternity. He is turning us into a church that truly is beautiful beyond description, his glorious bride, adorned in the white linen of Christ's perfect obedience.

Costly Love

Make no mistake, this transformation is a costly renovation project for God. In order to make his church into an awe-inspiring, holy city, filled with glorious saints, God had to take into himself all our filth and self-centered refusal to love others faithfully. Jesus had to leave the glory and unchanging perfection of heaven and enter this dark world of broken, unfaithful people. Surrounded by unfaithful disciples, who constantly fought among themselves, tried to correct Jesus' perspectives on his own ministry, and finally abandoned him and fled, Jesus nonetheless loved them faithfully to the end. Whereas we might have exclaimed to the disciples, "That's it! I've had it with you!," Jesus said, "This is the cup that I came to drink, the cup that means judgment for me so that we can share the cup of blessing in all eternity." Jesus also welcomed people who had no loveliness in themselves to come to him. He showed kindness to the woman of Samaria, a member of a hated minority, who was an outcast even from her own group because of her serial sexual unfaithfulness (John 4). He affirmed her, too, in all her brokenness and sin, as someone whom his Father was seeking as a worshiper. He had indeed come to seek and to save those who were lost—even lost and unfaithful people such as you and me.

What is more, Jesus Christ remained faithful to the very end. In order to restore our shattered relationship with God, Jesus had to endure a terrible break in his own relationship with the Father. Because we have repeatedly closed the door in God's face, the Father closed the door in judgment on his own Son, turning away the glorious light of his shining face from Jesus, so that there was a thick, impenetrable darkness between them. Far from a welcoming smile, Jesus endured the Father's deepest wrath and anger—all the wrath and anger that we deserved. That is why, even though we have failed God repeatedly in the way we have pursued our own relationships, selfishly using and then discarding people when they no longer suited us, we can still come back to God. When we return, tremblingly wondering whether there is any hope for us, we discover that God's arms are still open wide for us, his smile is toward us, and his faithful love still welcomes us back. We are not merely seated in a chariot with nobility; we are seated in glory with the King of kings, included in a new and glorious kingdom and crowned with hope of a still greater glory that is yet to come, when we see him face to face. How incredible to hear of such grace extended to us!

Perhaps you have never yet experienced this joy. You are still wondering what God's attitude toward you will be if you come to him. Wonder no more! God welcomes you with open arms. Or perhaps you have been welcomed many times before, but have found yourself wandering away yet again. Come back to the garden of your first love, and discover that the flowers of God's love for you are indeed still in bloom. Your heavenly Spouse has never abandoned his first and eternal love for you, and he never will. He awaits you in his garden with great joy. Be amazed and celebrate that joy afresh, as you ponder the awesome grace and unique faithfulness of Jesus Christ to you, and look forward to the completion of his sanctifying work, in you and in all those whom you love.

10

And So (Once More) to Bed . . .

Song of Songs 6:11—8:4

Woman
11 I went down to a garden of walnut trees,
to look at the shoots of the valley,
to see if the vine had budded
and the pomegranates were in bloom.
12 I don't know what's up with me.
You set me in chariots with a nobleman.

Man
13 Return, return, O Perfect One;
return, return, so that we may gaze upon you.
How you gaze on the Perfect One,
like on the dance of two camps!

7:1 How beautiful are your feet in sandals,
[like the] daughter of a noble!
The curves of your hips are like ornaments
made by the hands of a craftsman.
2 Your navel is a rounded bowl;
may it not lack mixed wine;
your belly is a heap of wheat,
bordered by lilies.

3 Your two breasts are like two fawns,
twins of the gazelle.
4 Your neck is like a tower of ivory;
your eyes are pools in Heshbon,
by the gate of Bath-rabbim.
Your nose is like the tower of Lebanon,
keeping watch towards Damascus.
5 Your head upon you is like [Mount] Carmel,
and the hair of your head is like purple;
a king could be bound by the tresses.
6 How beautiful you are and how pleasant, love,
the daughter of pleasures!
7 Your stature is like a palm tree,
and your breasts are like clusters of dates.
8 I said, "I will climb up the palm tree,
I will seize its date blossoms.
May your breasts be like clusters on the vine,
and the fragrance of your breath be like apples."
9 Your palate is like the best wine . . .

Woman
. . . flowing smoothly for my beloved,
gliding past sleeping lips.
10 I am my beloved's,
and his desire is towards me.

11 Come, my love,
let us go out to the field;
let us spend the night among the henna bushes.
12 Let us get up early [and go] to the vineyards;
let us see if the vine has budded,
if the blossom clusters have opened,
if the pomegranates have bloomed.
There I will give my caresses to you.
13 The mandrakes emit their scent,
and beside our doorways are all of the choice fruits,
new and old, my love,
[which] I have treasured up for you.

8:1 Oh that you were my brother,
who nursed at the breasts of my mother.
When I found you in the street, I would kiss you,
and no one would despise me.
2 I would lead you; I would bring you
to the house of my mother who taught me;
I would give you spiced wine to drink,
the juice of my pomegranate.
3 May his left hand be under my head,
and his right hand embrace me!
4 I charge you, daughters of Jerusalem,
that you will absolutely not arouse or awaken love
until it delights.

It is quite an achievement to write a commentary on the Song of Songs and not talk about sex at all. Some people manage it, though. Interpreters of the more allegorical persuasion have read this passage and talked about the woman's belly as representing the fruitfulness of the church in producing offspring for Christ and her breasts as symbolizing the good food of the Word with which those children are sustained. In his introduction to the Song of Songs, Matthew Henry advises readers to "forget that we have bodies," which seems an apt description of this approach.[1]

God does not forget that we have bodies. After all, he was the One who carefully designed those bodies and chose to give them to us. It is Greek philosophy, not the Bible, that sees the body as evil and the soul alone as spiritual and valuable. God is concerned about the body and what we do with our bodies. So God is willing to do what some commentators are not: to talk to us about our bodies and our sexuality. God is not embarrassed by such subjects, and neither should we be embarrassed by them. Equally, though, the Word of God is not crass and crude when it talks about sex. It treats the body with an appropriate poetic modesty and restraint that we should try to respect.

Perfect!

When we left our couple at the end of the previous chapter, they were in the midst of making up after a fight. The woman had gone down to the

1. Quoted in Douglas Sean O'Donnell, *Song of Solomon*, Preaching the Word (Wheaton, IL: Crossway, 2012), 97.

garden of her love to see whether a few blossoms had survived the chilly winter of her frosty coldness toward her husband (Song 6:11). What she discovered when she got there astonished her. The man received her back without recriminations or scolding, expressing again his unique and committed love to her alone. She was caught up into the clouds in raptures, as if she had been plucked from the crowd to ride in state with a nobleman in a parade (v. 12). She was flying high!

That is where this passage begins, with him calling her back to earth. It is as though he were saying, "Hey! Get out of your chariot with your nobleman and come back to *me*! Come back here so that I can gaze at your perfection." Literally, he calls her *Shulammite*, which some have taken to be her name, or the place where she is from. But I think it is better understood as a title drawn from the word *shalom*, which means "peace" or "wholeness." She is the perfect one for him, the one who brings him peace and wholeness (see Song 8:10).

What is more, the woman's perfection includes every inch of her body. In his earlier words affirming her beauty, the man omitted references to her lips and her body below her neck because their fight had been over sex, and he hadn't wanted to give her the impression that he was interested in making up simply so that he could get her back into bed. Now that their relationship is restored, however, he has no such inhibitions. He describes her body from the soles of her feet upward, rather than in the more common direction from the head downward. Apart from the sandals that adorn her feet, he doesn't mention any items of clothing interrupting his view. Her feet are like the daughter of a noble, soft and dainty, rather than the coarse and work-calloused feet of a peasant woman, which is why she needs sandals (Song 7:1). The Hebrew word for *feet* here, *pa'am*, normally indicates feet that are in motion and suggests the gracefulness of her steps as she moves like a dancer, though it is not necessary to conclude that she is actually dancing here.

The next four items—hips, navel, belly, and breasts—are linked together by their rounded shape and association with sex and fertility. The "curves of [her] hips" (Song 7:1) are the curves at the upper part of her legs, hence her bottom. These curves are compared to ornaments made by a skilled "craftsman," a word that recalls the description in the book of Proverbs of wisdom as a craftsman working alongside God at creation. This points toward God's role in designing the glories of the feminine body. Her "navel" is a rounded cup containing spiced wine (v. 2). This is probably a discreet euphemism for the lower part of her abdomen, since otherwise we would expect the navel to come after the belly. Comparing it to a cup containing spiced wine alludes to the intoxicating pleasures that this area of her anatomy contains for her lover. Love—more specifically, "sexual caresses"—is often compared to wine in the Song (e.g., 1:2), but this is no ordinary wine. It is a particularly special wine, supplemented with sweeteners and aromatic scents.

Next the man describes her belly as a rounded heap of wheat (Song 7:2)—the exact opposite of the flat stomach for which modern women and men so often strive. Wheat and wine were staple foods for the population, so an abundance of these things signifies the rich blessing of fertility. The Hebrew word for *belly* also indicates the womb, and it would appear that here, as in many other cultures, ancient tastes preferred women to look well fed and slightly pregnant rather than as though they were in imminent danger of starvation.

The particular heap of wheat that represents her belly, though, is surrounded by lilies (Song 7:2). At first sight, this may seem a jarring juxtaposition, since in the real world lilies would hardly grow around a heap of wheat. Within the world of the poem, though, lilies have already been used to describe his lips (5:13) and her breasts (4:5). The combination of wheat and lilies stresses the fact that her belly is valued not simply for its ability to bear children but for its sensuality as well. In comparing her breasts to twin fawns (7:3), the images of fertility and sexual enjoyment likewise overlap and overflow into one another. He doesn't simply want the woman as the mother of his children; he wants her for herself.

The woman is not just an objectified body, however, as in pornographic representations of the female form. The man describes five elements of her upper body—neck, eyes, nose, head, and hair—to balance the five parts of her lower body. Her neck is like a tower of ivory (Song 7:4), slender and upright. This indicates that she holds herself with dignity and pride and has no need to drop her head in shame. Her eyes are like pools of water (v. 4), clear and shining, just as his were earlier compared to doves beside the water (5:12). Her nose is like the tower of Lebanon (7:4)—not literally in size and shape, of course, but representing the fact that she looks down confidently on all dangers, here summed up by Damascus, the capital city of Israel's ancient foes, the Arameans. Her head is held upright like Mount

Carmel, while her hair is as valuable as purple (v. 5). Purple was the most precious of ancient dyes, since it was derived through a costly process of collecting and crushing tiny sea snails. Her hair is almost an active part of her, able to hold a king captive in its flowing tresses (v. 5). Once again, there is a military background to several of these metaphors, underlining her dignity, security, and awe-inspiring character. This image of womanly perfection is no compliant plastic doll who exists simply to do the man's bidding. She retains the powerful strength of character that we saw depicted in the previous passage. She is a living, breathing, awe-inspiring piece of God's handiwork from the soles of her feet to the top of her head.

I Will Climb the Tree

At this point, the image shifts from depicting the woman in terms of architecture and mountains to a tall date palm tree, with her breasts as the bunches of dates (Song 7:7–8). This reflects a progression in the man's desire, from merely beholding her beauty to wanting to touch and delight in her pleasures. He longs to climb the palm tree and pick her dates—to play with her breasts and taste the sweet wine of her kisses and caresses. This time the man doesn't have to ask twice; in fact, the woman is so eager to oblige him that she breaks into his speech and finishes his sentence for him.[2] She doesn't roll her eyes and say, "Stop thinking about sex all the time." Rather, she exults in the fact that her body is his and that he desires her sexually. Significantly, the Hebrew word for *desire* here (*tešûqâ*) is the same rare word that appears in Genesis 3:16, where it describes the woman's disordered desire for her husband that contributes to conflict between the sexes. Here, though, it refers to the man's proper desire for her, emphasizing the mutuality of their longing for each other and the new peace that they have found in each other.

In words that echo the language at the end of chapter 1, the woman suggests that they should go out into the open country, to find an idyllic setting where they can enjoy exploring the blossoms of their love together (Song 7:11). The metaphors run together and overflow, picking up on earlier poems to stress both their mutual enjoyment of sexual love and the

2. The shift in speakers is easier to see in Hebrew, in which the second-person pronouns are marked for gender.

joyful prospect of offspring that it brings. For them as a married couple, sex is a delightful enjoyment of "choice fruits, new and old" (v. 13), not just a routine exercise. It breathes the perfumed air of their garden of love. The mention of mandrakes and pomegranates among those fruits, though, reminds us of the pervasive presence of the language of fertility that underlies the poem, for both were associated with childbearing in the ancient world. In a passage that has already referenced the opening chapters of Genesis, the choice fruits of their love inevitably include the anticipation of the blessing of fruitfulness that the Lord pronounced on the original couple in Eden.

The woman remembers, however, that there are social boundaries that need to be observed. Even as a married couple, they cannot simply kiss in the street (Song 8:1). They could not even show the same level of public affection that a brother and sister would be able to demonstrate without inviting social disapprobation.[3] She longs for them to be in private, not merely in the outdoors but at her mother's house. This was the place to which she longed to bring the man when she found him back in chapter 3. If she could bring him home to Mom, it would be a sign that their relationship had the stamp of parental approval. In chapter 3, it was a wish that could not yet be fulfilled. Now, though, it is not merely a frustrating wish. She can finally bring him home to the place of social acceptance, where she can put into practice all the wonderful insights that her mother taught her, which she coyly describes as giving him spiced wine to drink, the juice of her pomegranate (8:2). This may put a whole new perspective on Paul's admonition in Titus 2:3–4 that the older women should teach the younger women!

She concludes her speech, returning to the cautionary note that we have seen several times before: Daughters of Jerusalem, this is why it is really important to wait to stir up love (Song 8:4). Love includes powerful sexual desires that cannot be satisfied with a polite sisterly embrace in the street. If you stir up love too soon, before there is an appropriate opportunity to follow through on those urges in a context of which even your mother would approve, the result will be either intense frustration or giving in to those urges outside of marriage. Like all other sin, sex outside of mar-

3. Gianni Barbiero, *Song of Songs: A Close Reading*, trans. Michael Tait, SVT 144 (Leiden: Brill, 2011), 425.

riage leads to guilt and shame, rather than the joy and satisfaction that it pretends to offer.

The Power of Praise

This poem underlines again the power of positive words. Of course, the depiction of the woman in the poem is idealized, and none of us possess such perfect bodies. Yet it would be a mistake to think that true love either requires or ignores physical beauty. The power in the man's speech comes from the fact that to him, the woman really is a picture of perfection—body and soul, outside and inside. To him, she is the Shulammite, the perfect one who completes him. For the poem (and the relationship!) to work, the man genuinely has to feel that way. To say these things if he didn't mean them would be utter hypocrisy. Yet at the same time, he doesn't have to examine her from the perspective of a judge at a modeling agency in order for the poem to have power. She doesn't have to be Helen of Troy—beautiful to all who behold her. She simply has to be beautiful *to him*.

In the same way, physical attraction between men and women is important. You ought to be able to say sincerely to your beloved on your wedding day, "You are truly beautiful." And you should repeat those words often in your marriage. Never tire of declaring your beloved's charms, for sincere words of affirmation have tremendous power to evoke and nourish love. Yet it is also thankfully true, in God's providence, that men and women can be attracted to all kinds of body shapes and sizes, and to every different personality type under the sun. Don't assume, therefore, that if you don't fit the cultural picture of perfect beauty—perhaps because your nose really does look like the Tower of Lebanon—the experience described in this poem is not for you. Human beauty really is in the eyes of the beholder, and even in the case of this woman, it is her character as much as her physique that the man finds profoundly attractive.

The Joy of Married Sex

What is more, the poem declares loudly the message of the delightfulness of married sex. Conventional wisdom in our culture bombards us on all sides in movies and television commercials asserting that random encounters with strangers are far more exciting and passionate. It claims that sex is just a physical experience, and that sex without commitment is less complicated and more fun, to be enjoyed wherever and whenever the opportunity presents itself. This is plainly nonsense. In marriage are delightful treasures, new and old, that make (or at least ought to make) married sex far better than anything you can find outside of marriage. In marriage, you get to know and trust each other intimately and therefore can learn exactly what pleases the other person. Moreover, within marriage, sex functions as a profound part of a relationship, not as a substitute for one. According to contemporary culture, Solomon and his concubines ought to have had the greatest sex, but if sex after a conflict has been resolved is as great as this passage suggests, then Solomon really was missing out on something terrific. The reality is that sex is too good to be wasted on anyone other than your spouse.

Yet if our culture has argued that sex is just for fun and has nothing to do with making babies, sometimes in Christian circles people have responded by arguing that sex is just about babies and not about pleasure. In fact, we sometimes give the impression that we can't possibly talk about sex because we're Christians. Mothers are often not teaching their daughters anything about this subject, let alone useful counsel on how they may best please their husbands, and fathers are equally reticent in teaching their sons. As a result, young people are left to learn about sex from *Cosmopolitan* or *Playboy* magazine, sources that are unlikely to convey biblical wisdom on the subject. This is perhaps the inevitable consequence of hundreds of years of the church's reading the Song of Songs while forgetting that we have bodies.

A proper reading of the Song strikes a beautiful balance between the extremes of viewing sex as simply for pleasure and seeing it as simply for childbearing. On the one hand, there is a tremendous celebration of fertility and great joy in the prospect of bearing godly offspring in this passage, as there is in the rest of the Bible. This is yet another reason why sex belongs firmly grounded in the context of marriage. If you are not ready to have children with the person you are sleeping with, you have no business sleeping with him or her in the first place. Indeed, this is one of the questions to ask yourself at an early point in a relationship: "Is this the man I want to be the father of my children?" or "Will she be a great mother for my kids?"

Yet at the same time, marriage is not just a means to have children. Some couples are unable to have children, yet can nonetheless have vibrant and joyful marriages in which they comfort and support one another through that painful experience, as well as finding other avenues of fruitful service in God's kingdom. The man was made to delight in the woman's body and vice versa as the source of wonderful pleasures, whether or not in God's providence these pleasures result in children. Satan did not invent our sexual desires. Our bodies were designed by God with all their differences to be intriguing and enchanting to our spouses. Sex was invented by God to be delightful in its own right as a way to bless your spouse and for him or her to bless you. It wasn't intended to be fun for men and a necessary nuisance for women; on the contrary, it was supposed from the beginning to be a mutually enriching experience of great joy for both.

Yet if sex is so great, does it mean that single people are missing out and living second-class lives? The passage clearly teaches the wisdom of waiting until marriage for sex. Some things in life are worth waiting for. At the same time, the most fulfilled human being who ever lived, Jesus Christ, was single and never had sex. So it is not as though single people are somehow deficient and incomplete without marriage, nor is it true that they cannot have meaningful and profound relationships with other singles and with married people. God didn't design us to live life on our own, whether we are married or single, but rather to be bonded together in community in the church, where we love and serve one another in deep and profound ways.

Sexual Sin and Shame

The beauty of the sexual relationship depicted in this poem presses painfully in on all of us—whether single or married—the brokenness of our own sexuality. None of us attain to this glorious picture of our sexuality, and the result of our failure is that our experience of sex and sexual desire is often dominated by profound shame rather than by deep joy. For some of us, that shame comes from the fact that our desire is toward people that it ought not to be toward, or because it is fulfilled in ways that are out of accord with God's design. Perhaps we objectify members of the same or of the opposite sex and lust after them, using them to fulfill the sinful desires of our hearts, rather than loving and serving them. Perhaps we habitually view pornography, or deliberately use our own bodies to attract the eyes of others. Some struggle with particular patterns of sexual sin or brokenness because of the past sins of others against them.

Because our sexual sin is rooted and grounded in our hearts, it easily moves from our eyes and our minds to our bodies in various forms of promiscuity. Sometimes we pursue bodily attractiveness and sex as idols in themselves, while at other times we use them to feed our other idolatries. We may say to ourselves, "If people find me attractive and compliment my looks, then I am worthwhile," or "If I sleep with my boyfriend, then he will stay with me, and I will have that relationship that makes me a valuable person," or even "I slept with my girlfriend, so now I have to stay with her to prove that I am not a failure as a Christian." We may develop eating disorders or spend many hours at the gym as we pursue the body shape that our culture insists is most beautiful, or we may disfigure or hide our bodies because of fear of sex or to punish ourselves for past sexual issues. Because our sexual desires are so strong, and we live in a culture that excels in stirring them up in all kinds of contexts where they cannot be properly satisfied, it is hardly surprising that so many of us struggle with these things.

What is more, if we do not personally struggle at present with our sexual desires, we may puff ourselves up with pride that we are not like "those people" all around us. In terms of Jesus' parable of the lost son (Luke 15:11–32), we may easily become sexual elder brothers and sisters, looking down our noses in judgment at the prodigal siblings around us, not realizing that whatever purity we may possess in this area is a gift of God's grace, not an attainment of our personal strength and holiness.

Even as married people, we find that our sexuality is often not the blessing that it was intended to be. Sometimes we use sex as a weapon, to purchase something from our spouse or to punish him or her for some offense. At other times, we may be resentful of our spouse's desire or lack of desire, viewing our bodies as our own possession, not as belonging to our husband or our wife. Instead of bonding us together in a glorious, joyful, and unique union, sex easily becomes a battleground in which we fight for our rights and seek to get our own way at all costs. That is why Paul had to remind the Corinthians that husbands and wives should give each other conjugal rights freely; the wife does not have authority over her own body, and neither does the husband over his. Their bodies belong to their spouses (1 Cor. 7:3–4). Instead of the blessing of the Song of Songs—"I am my beloved's, and his desire is for me" (Song 7:10 ESV)—we experience the pain of the curse of Genesis 3:16: "Your desire shall be for your husband, and he shall rule over you."

The bitter truth is that we are all profoundly broken in body and soul, and perhaps that is nowhere clearer than in our sexuality. As a result of the fall, even those who succeed in attaining great physical beauty and acquiring all the sex they want will lose both in the end. In the long run, beauty really is vain and charm deceiving, as Proverbs 31:30 declares. The perfect bodies that are described in the Song of Songs will eventually grow wrinkly and sag in key places. The lovers that we pursue inevitably lose their attractiveness and/or lose interest in us. Even the best and most loving spouses eventually grow old and die, if we don't die ourselves first. Our idols curse our failures far more than they bless our successes, leading to lives that are frequently dogged by frustration, shame, depression, and despair.

Sex Is Not Enough

What this means is that sex, even great sex within a wonderful marriage, is not enough. A stunningly beautiful body is not enough. We need a better Husband, who gives us a perfect beauty, in which he then delights—an eternal Husband who loves us with an intensity of passion of which human sexuality is only a pale reflection. We all long to be loved, and not just in the way that an affectionate brother loves us, greeting us in the street with a peck on the cheek. We want to be loved by somebody who longs for us with a powerful and frightening hunger: we long to be ravished by love. As John Donne put it:

> Take me to you, imprison me, for I,
> Except you enthrall me, never shall be free,
> Nor ever chaste, except you ravish me.[4]

Ravishing love is exactly what we encounter in the gospel. In the book of Ezekiel, the Lord describes his loving provision for his bride, Jerusalem (Ezek. 16). Finding her helpless, ugly, and naked at birth, he protected her and adorned her with exquisite jewelry to highlight her beauty. Yet she spurned his faithful love and went after her idols, seeking her security

4. John Donne, "Holy Sonnets, 14," in *The Complete English Poems* (London: Penguin, 1977), 315.

and value in relationships with foreign nations. She took all the gifts that the Lord had given her and spent them on pursuing her lovers. Such acts led to her judgment for her sins and the destruction of Jerusalem at the hands of the Babylonians. Yet in spite of Israel's persistent unfaithfulness, God's love would not let her go. Instead, Ezekiel goes on to explain how Jerusalem, too, would be restored, alongside her sisters in sin, Samaria (the notorious home of religious sin) and Sodom (the notorious home of sexual and social sin).

How is it possible for a trio of such perverse sisters to be restored to fellowship with a holy God? Wouldn't eternal judgment be a more fitting fate for people like that—and indeed, for people like us? It would be, apart from the powerful and frightening intensity of God's love—a love that will not let his people go. Only such love explains the cross. Only such love accounts for the Father's pouring out the fullness of his wrath against *our* sin—sexual and otherwise—on his own Son. Only such love accounts for Jesus' giving his body to be so racked with pain and agony that he scarcely looked human, and certainly had no beauty to draw people to him. Only such love explains the Father's gently removing our torn and stained apparel, wiping away our tears of shame, and then reclothing us in the festival garments of Christ's righteousness, to make us ready for the wedding of the Lamb. Only such love adequately describes the power of God's desire to have a pure and holy bride for his Son, a people who will belong to him, body and soul, for all eternity. Those whom he has chosen *must* be part of his bride.

The Answer for Our Shame

How will you respond to your own sexual brokenness? Maybe you are resolving once again to do better in the future. Perhaps you are planning to guard your eyes, heart, and body better than you have done thus far. Those are good resolutions, but none of us has the power to make ourselves pure. Many of us have found that our sexual desires have far greater power than we can easily resist. If we were to count how many times in an average day our thoughts drifted into sexual sin, we might be overwhelmed with guilt.

Perhaps you are overwhelmed with guilt as you read this, feeling that you are the worst Christian that there is—or not even a Christian at all—because of your sins in this area. Often, the church gives the impression that sexual sin is one of the worst possible transgressions. As a result, we tend to hide these sins in dark corners, instead of confessing them openly at the cross, where we can receive help, counsel, and forgiveness. The truth is that though it can certainly have serious immediate consequences for our lives, from an eternal perspective sexual sin is no different from any other kind of sin. Jesus drew to himself many people who were notorious for their sexual brokenness and provided them with the forgiveness that they needed, washing away their guilt. There was the woman who was caught in the very act of adultery (John 8); the woman of Samaria who had had five husbands and was living with a man who wasn't her husband (John 4); the notorious woman who came and washed Jesus' feet with her tears (Luke 7). He never shamed these people or condemned them for their sin; indeed, he was willing to have his own reputation reviled in order to provide them with cleansing, acceptance, a new life, and a new hope.

Join these people who came to Jesus with their sin. Bring your broken sexual history to Jesus, whatever its exact nature—lust, pornography, the pursuit of same-sex desires, premarital sex, adultery, or some other sin. Bring it to the foot of the cross and lay it down there. Let God nail it to the cross with Jesus Christ, as part of the record of sins that he died for, and that he paid for in full. Then hear the glorious words that Jesus says about *your* sin: "It is finished. It is paid for. It is done away with. See, your guilt is taken away and your iniquity is atoned for. You are set free to learn to truly love your brothers and your sisters. You are released to live life, to continue to wrestle against temptation, sometimes winning, perhaps often losing, but always looking to the cross as your only hope in life and death. My righteousness is enough for you."

Jesus Christ has loved his bride perfectly. Although we have no beauty or holiness to attract him to us, he has loved us since before time began and will love us when time is finally done. He will bring us to his Father's house so that we may spend a joy-filled eternity delighting in his glory, enraptured by his beauty, astonished by the old and new treasures of his grace. We will behold him, and that sight will be enough to make up for whatever difficulties and challenges lie between now and then. But still more amazing, Jesus Christ will spend a joy-filled eternity delighting in his bride's glory, enraptured by the beauty of the holiness that he has created in us, thrilled by the fruit that has been borne by the old and new treasures of his grace.

For the joy that was set before him, Jesus endured the cross, scorning its shame, and so he will rejoice forever in the joy of his beloved, then clothed in fine linen, glorious in holy array, shining like the sun. On that day, he will say, "Come, my beloved, my perfect one, how beautiful you are! You are mine and I am yours forever!"

11

Love and Death

Song of Songs 8:5–7

Daughters of Jerusalem
5 Who is this coming up from the wilderness,
supporting herself upon her beloved?

Woman
Under the apple tree, I aroused you;
there your mother conceived you;
there she conceived,
she who brought you forth.
6 Set me like a seal upon your heart,
like a seal upon your arm.
For love is as strong as Death,
jealousy is as intense as Sheol.
Its flames are flames of fire,
an Almighty flame!
7 Many waters are not able to extinguish love,
and rivers cannot drown it.
Even if a man should give all the wealth of his house as the price of love,
he would be utterly scorned.

What is love? There are plenty of potential answers to that question in the world of popular culture. According to the rock singer Pat Benatar, love is a battlefield.[1] Many of us can relate to that perspective, especially those who have been married for a while. Just as no one has the same power to bless and encourage you as your spouse, so, too, no one else has the power of a spouse to provoke, exasperate, or even hurt you deeply. Love is not an easy pathway to tread.

On the other hand, if you believe singer Bette Midler, love is a seed hiding beneath the "bitter snows" that when exposed to the sunshine in the spring will finally become a rose.[2] As a gardener, I find that analogy horticulturally suspect. The chances of someone's planting a seed in the fall and getting a rose in the spring are about on a par with finding Jack's magic beans that grow into a cloud-rending beanstalk. In the real world, roses are grafted onto existing stems and bought from nurseries, not grown from seed. But if we may deconstruct Ms. Midler, perhaps that is precisely the point of the song: love is beautiful and desirable but in the end ultimately elusive, as legendary and hard to find in this broken world as leprechauns, unicorns—and roses grown from seed. Some can probably relate to that perspective on love as well. Maybe you find it emotionally difficult to attend weddings, because when you watch the bride and groom's love for each other, you find it hard to imagine that something like that could ever happen for you.

Another definition of love comes from Bruce Lee, the master of martial arts, who once observed:

> Love is like a friendship caught on fire. In the beginning a flame, very pretty, often hot and fierce, but still only light and flickering. As love grows older, our hearts mature and our love becomes as coals, deep-burning and unquenchable.[3]

I don't know if Mr. Lee ever read the Bible, but "friendship caught on fire" is a good summary of the love that we have seen described in the Song of Songs. Yet there are aspects of the other definitions in the passage as well. Fire is very pretty, but the coals can burn as well as warm; a rose is one of the most beautiful of flowers, but roses have thorns as well as blooms; battlefields can be places of memorable triumphs, but battlefields can also be scenes of bitter defeat and awful death. So, too,

1. Pat Benatar, "Love Is a Battlefield," written by Holly McKnight and Mike Chapman © 1983 Chrysalis Records.

2. Bette Midler, "The Rose," written by Amanda McBroom © 1979 Atlantic Records.

3. Bruce Lee, *Artist of Life*, ed. John Little (Boston: Tuttle, 1999), 96.

throughout the Song, we have seen the most glorious descriptions of love side by side with stern warnings against stirring up love too soon. In this passage, as we reach the poetic climax of the Song, the glory and pain of love are once again starkly portrayed side by side in a series of distinct but related images.

Who Is This Coming Up from the Wilderness?

The passage begins with the woman coming up from the wilderness (Song 8:5). This is the second time in the Song that we have heard the exclamation "Who is this coming up from the wilderness?" Last time, in chapter 3, it described the woman coming to meet her beloved for their wedding. Now, at the end of the poem, it depicts her once again coming up from the wilderness. This time she is no longer alone, though: she is leaning on the arm of her beloved. Love starts its sequence with the wedding march, in which the woman emerges from the wilderness—the place of wandering, danger, and death—and comes to the safety of the promised land, accompanied and protected by her beloved. This is one beautiful image for love: a journey that leads from loneliness, emptiness, and chaos into a new life of blessing and hope.

The second image depicts the woman gazing at an apple tree (Song 8:5). In chapter 2, in a passage where she spoke frankly of her desire to sleep with the man, the woman described the man as an apple tree under whose shade she desired to sit and whose fruit she longed to eat. Here the metaphor is shifted slightly: the apple tree is now described as the place where she first aroused her lover. What she told the daughters of Jerusalem not to do until it was ready—arouse love—is exactly what she did at the right time with the man.[4] Because they waited until the appropriate season, their first union under the apple tree is a joyful memory, without need for guilt, remorse, or regret. Here is the second element in the sequence of love: sex, which appropriately takes place after marriage.

4. With its clear sexual overtones, this is a particularly hard passage for those who wish to interpret the Song allegorically or typologically. In order to interpret the "awakening" here as the Christian seeking Christ's help through prayer, James Durham argued that Christ is *both* the man and the apple tree in this passage. *The Song of Solomon* (1668; repr., Edinburgh: Banner of Truth; 1982), 416. Meanwhile, Christopher Mitchell sees the woman as representing Christ, as he is present in the church. *The Song of Songs* (St. Louis: Concordia, 2003), 422. Both attempts seem to result in very strained interpretations of the text.

Even in its proper context, though, the apple tree of sexual love still has its own pains—in this case, the ones that come with childbirth. The apple tree where she aroused him is, she says, the same place where his own mother labored in childbirth with him (Song 8:5). This statement should not be taken literally, of course. People didn't normally give birth to children under trees in antiquity any more than they do now. But the apple tree is a poetic reminder that love and marriage generally do lead to the joy and the pain of childbirth: the outrageous joy of having a child to carry on the family line, which was at the same time intimately united with the excruciating pain of childbirth without the benefit of modern anesthetics. Pain in childbirth was part of the curse on humanity that resulted from the fall (Gen. 3:16). Ever since that time, love and pain belong inextricably together as one generation succeeds the next. This, then, is the third element in the sequence: marriage, sex, babies.

Yet there is more to life than weddings, sex, and babies. Love is not just a sweet union of two souls journeying peacefully from the wilderness into the promised land of family life. It is a lifelong and unique commitment, an insatiable appetite that cannot be tamed, placated, bought, or sold. We have seen some of these challenges on our journey through the Song of Songs. Love demands to possess its beloved and to be possessed by him in a unique way. This is expressed by the woman's desire to become a seal on the man's heart and on his arm (Song 8:6). In antiquity, seals were among a person's most precious possessions. They were used to sign documents and to mark ownership of precious objects. In those days, if you wanted to steal someone's identity, you didn't steal his credit cards; you stole his seal. So when the woman says that she wants to be like a seal that her beloved carries around his arm, the place of his strength, she wants to be constantly beside him, publicly acknowledged as belonging to him.

Yet the woman doesn't merely want to be carried beside the man like one of his possessions. She also wants to be within him, like a seal imprinted on the soft clay of his heart, constantly in his thoughts and in his affections. The woman wants to be everything to him, inside and out, physically, emotionally, and spiritually. In fact, since seals were used to mark ownership, what she is saying is that she wants to own him, not simply to belong to him. The previous verse depicted her coming up from the wilderness at their wedding, leaning on her beloved; the image of the seal describes her longing that their relationship remain inextricably bonded and exclusively committed, until death parts them.

Love as Strong as Death

Death is the only image powerful enough to be compared to such love. Love is not merely as strong as an ox, or as powerful as a speeding locomotive: it is as strong as *death* (Song 8:6). Just as people who enter the fierce grip of death do not emerge again, so, too, having entered the equally powerful realm of love, the woman wants love to grip them both forever. She wants their relationship to remain exclusive and unique, as unyielding and relentless in its single-minded jealousy as the parallel image of Sheol, the grave. Death doesn't take bribes, nor can anyone buy more time for life by distracting the grave's attention. The grave never loses its single-minded focus on swallowing people up. So, too, the poet says, is the woman's jealousy.

We usually think of jealousy as a negative emotion, a refusal to share something that ought to be shared. Perhaps we get jealous if someone else is getting the attention that we think we deserve or if another person acquires something that we really desire. Indeed, we spend a lot of time and effort teaching our children not to be jealous, but to share. They need to let their little brother play with their toys and to rejoice when their sister gets a present that they wish they had. I vividly remember that one Christmas when I was about seven, my great-aunt gave me a plastic model kit of a World War II battleship to construct, while my sisters got cute stuffed animals. I was furiously angry and vented my feelings on all around me. I was sinfully jealous, even though my great-aunt had actually put considerable thought into providing me with a suitable gift.

But some things in life are not meant to be shared. When our kids were small, they were adorable. Yet if you had come to Barb and me and asked if you could buy them, or even just borrow them for a year or two, we would have said no. We were jealous over our children, conscious that God had given us the unique calling to raise them. We would not share the privilege of parenting them with other people. In the same way, there is an appropriate jealousy in marriage. You belong uniquely to the other person and he or she belongs to you. This doesn't mean that you have to be together for every second of every day and can never speak to members of the opposite sex without your spouse's permission. We were never intended to meet all the relational needs of our spouses, and it would be folly to try. But loving someone means that you have a unique relationship with your spouse, who holds your heart in his or her hands in a special way that no one else shares. No one else should know your struggles in the way that your spouse does. No one else should delight in your triumphs and joys the way your spouse does. Some things are not meant to be shared.

Love Is a Divine Fire

The woman also compares love to a flaming fire—not just any fire, but a blaze as intense as the flames of the Almighty, the Lord himself.[5] Married love is not merely a comfortable companionship. Otherwise, we could be married to many people at the same time, just as we can have many friends. Married love is more than friendship. It is a mutual, exclusive commitment: friendship on fire. It is this aspect of fiery longing in marriage that the Song of Songs brings out so powerfully. The Song describes the desire of each man and woman to possess a unique and lastingly committed soulmate who will be not only friend but lover, someone who is madly and passionately devoted to that one person and to him or her alone. This is why proposing marriage to someone is not just a matter of calmly explaining to your intended the various strengths that you and she bring to the table and proposing a corporate merger. Marriage is intended to be a flaming, red-hot relationship.

This is a countercultural expectation, to say the least. Our culture still desires burning passion, but has largely disconnected marriage from that expectation. Our society's image for marriage is built around the model of Tevye and Golde from *The Fiddler on the Roof.* In that musical, reflecting on twenty-five years of marriage, Tevye asks his wife, Golde, if she loves him. In response, she reminds him that she has washed his clothes, cooked his meals, cleaned his house, shared his bed, given him children, and milked his

5. Translations are divided over whether take the abbreviation *yah* as shorthand for the divine name in Song 8:6 (ESV; NASB) or simply as a superlative ("a mighty flame," NIV; see also HCSB). If this is a reference to the divine name, then it would be the only one in the entire book, but since this is the climax of the Song, such a reference is appropriate. Certainly, there are other, more direct ways of expressing a superlative in Hebrew that would not evoke the Lord's name in quite the same way. Perhaps the most elegant translation, retaining something of the ambiguity of the original, is "an Almighty flame." J. Cheryl Exum, *Song of Songs: A Commentary*, OTL (Louisville, KY: Westminster John Knox, 2005), 254.

cow. After twenty-five years, why should they talk about love now? But when he presses the point, "Do you love me?," she finally concedes, "I suppose I do." This is most people's image of married love: a good marriage is not so much a matter of shared passion as it is of shared chores. Yet the Bible joins the two together and calls us to a marriage that is not merely friendship but friendship on fire. We are meant to say not simply "I suppose I love you," but "I love you with a burning love that is as strong as death and as jealous as the grave." We were made for this kind of friendship on fire.

Love's Final Triumph

Marriage, sex, babies, enduring faithfulness, and death. Is that all there is? Is love only as strong as death? Does Sheol win in the end? Not at all. The final image speaks of the inextinguishable nature of love (Song 8:7). Love cannot be swept away by many waters or drowned by deep floods. It bears all things, believes all things, hopes all things, and endures all things (1 Cor. 13:7). Death and the grave cannot have the final say in the matter. Love must win in the end.

What is more, a love of this kind cannot be bought. The alternative commercial model of love, epitomized by Solomon, involves a simple cost-benefit analysis. It supposes that you get what you pay for in life, and so to get a good wife, you must be willing to pay a great deal. If necessary, perhaps you should even be prepared to give all the wealth of your house to acquire one (Song 8:7). Yet love laughs at that calculus. True love cannot be bought, nor can it be bargained for, even at the highest of prices. Someone who pursues that route will inevitably end up as the object of pity—or, even worse, of scorn—from those who truly know love.

This passage thus sets a high bar for what to look for in a spouse. Don't settle for marriage to someone whose best quality is that he or she is willing and available. That person deserves better than that, and so do you. Only a rich and profound love—friendship on fire—can endure the trials of life in a fallen world. Marriage is not a walk in the park, or a pleasant sail on a summer's afternoon. If you love someone enough to marry him or her, then you will inevitably pass with that person through the turmoil of sickness, conflict, childbirth—or the painful inability to have a child—many mutual and individual disappointments, brokenness, tears, sorrow, and ultimately death itself. Marriage is indeed, as the old vows say, "for better or worse, for richer or for poorer, in sickness or in health, till death do us part."

Nothing less than friendship on fire will carry you through the challenges of caring for your spouse when he becomes unable to care for himself, or of forgiving your spouse when she sins against you in deep and profoundly painful ways, of enduring together through the bad times as well as the good. Of course, the intensity of that fire will vary over the course of a lifetime. At times it will be a raging blaze, while at others it will settle back into glowing embers; sometimes you might have to dig through the ashes to find a live coal. Feelings come and go. Yet if love is going to endure all things, we need a love that many waters cannot extinguish and floods cannot drown.

This passage also sets a high bar within marriage. You are to treat your spouse like a seal. That means that he or she is to be your most precious possession, to be treasured like a pearl of great price. It also suggests that a spouse is meant to leave a lasting imprint on your heart, touching the deepest core of your being. Do you view and treat your spouse in that way? Do you nurture, cherish, and protect your spouse with an appropriate jealousy, regarding his or her highest welfare as your single-minded concern, laying down your life for that person daily? It is sometimes easy for us men to imagine giving our lives for our wives in some dramatic gesture, for example, by shielding her body from a terrorist's bullets. Yet God far more often asks us to give our lives for our wives daily in much more mundane ways, for example, by taking care of the children so that she can go to a Bible study, washing the dishes, listening patiently to her talk about the troubles of her friends, and so on. Love graciously endures and shares in the little things, as well as giving itself in grand gestures.

The Greater Treasure

Even at its very best, though, human marriage cannot and will not ultimately satisfy the desire that God has built into our souls for friendship on fire. Marriage is wonderful, but it is not enough. It was never intended to be enough: if marriage is all that we have, even the best marriage in the world will not satisfy our craving for love. Nor are we incomplete people without marriage. After all, according to the Bible, marriage was made in the beginning to give us the primary picture of Christ's relationship with the church (Eph. 5). It is in our relationship with Christ that we truly find the friendship on fire that we all need.

This is wonderful news because in this fallen world, we do not all have great marriages. Some people are single and may remain so throughout their lives. Yet they, too, long for a friendship that is on fire and face the temptation to search for that fire in all kinds of illicit directions. This temptation may take the shape of the allure of sexual pleasure outside marriage, whether acted out or kept in our hearts and minds in the form of lust.

Those of us who are married also repeatedly fall very far short of the high standard set by Scripture. We may be wrongly jealous of our spouses when we should trust them, or we may settle into dull and humdrum relationships because we cannot be bothered to love our spouses with the kind of passion that the Song describes. It is hard work to love someone like that. Maybe you have never experienced such a fire in your marriage, or the fire has long since gone out. Perhaps your attempts to express love receive an angry response from your spouse or an icy-cold rebuff. Yet God is able to light or relight that fire in the coldest of contexts. Even the best marriages have many painful moments and difficult experiences. There are times in every marriage when the fire seems to have grown cold. We are all sinners who repeatedly wound one another, both with our carelessness and through deliberate acts. Yet in our relationship with Christ, there is a true and burning love that we can all experience, whether we are happily married, unhappily married, divorced, widowed, or single.

In Jesus, we truly experience friendship on fire. For Jesus to win his spouse, it was not enough for him merely to humble himself and come to earth to be our friend. If he had simply come into this world to model true friendship and to show us what that kind of love looked like, we would simply have been condemned all the more for our failure as friends. His perfection in being patient, being kind, keeping no record of wrongs, and so on with a people who were cold and unresponsive would simply have highlighted all the more our sin and failure. Jesus had to do far more than that in order to win us as his friends forever. As Jesus himself said, "Greater love has no one than this, that someone lay down his life for his friends" (John 15:13). Jesus didn't just live the life of perfect love to give us an example to follow; he lived it *for us*, in our place. Then, in order to pay the penalty for our sins and restore our broken friendship with God, Jesus went to the cross to atone for all our sins and failures, including our failure to truly love God and love one another, whether within our marriages and families or more broadly. At the cross, love deliberately entered the power of death. Love lay down and died. It was the ultimate sacrifice.

Is love merely as strong as death? Is love's jealous desire to own someone simply on a par with the power of the grave? We might think so, if all we had to go on were human experience. When a couple gets married, they pledge their love to each other until death. A couple may love each other passionately for fifty years, and then suddenly she is gone and he is left behind. Soon he, too, will die, and then what will happen to their love? Does death really win in the end? Does the grave gain the final victory?

For three days after Christ entered the tomb, the heavens held their breath, and watched and waited. But then Christ, the very embodiment of God's love, emerged triumphantly from the grave and conquered death forever. He came up from the wilderness of the tomb, with his chosen bride, his church, leaning radiantly on his arm. Because of that victory, God could say to his people in the book of Isaiah:

> Fear not, for I have redeemed you;
> I have called you by name, you are mine.
> When you pass through the waters, I will be with you;
> and through the rivers, they shall not overwhelm you;
> when you walk through fire you shall not be burned,
> and the flame shall not consume you.
> For I am the LORD your God,
> the Holy One of Israel, your Savior. (Isa. 43:1–3)

Because Christ is risen, Paul can exclaim:

> "O death, where is your victory?
> O death, where is your sting?"
>
> The sting of death is sin, and the power of sin is the law. But thanks be to God, who gives us the victory through our Lord Jesus Christ. (1 Cor. 15:55–57)

This incredible, passionate love story is what every page of the Bible is about. Isaiah's words about God's faithful love transcending rivers and floods were written for people who found themselves in exile for their sin, far away from the land they had been promised. So, too, God's friendship on fire pursues us right where we are, with all our lostness, brokenness, and coldness, with all our failures to love him and others, and all our sins both outside and within marriage. The Lord is jealously calling you to an exclusive relationship with him, whether for the first time or returning from a far country yet again. God does not merely tolerate your presence; he is not just mildly fond of you; he *loves* you with an incredible, passionate love. Through his amazing friendship on fire that took him to earth to endure the agony of the cross and a shameful death for you, Jesus Christ has done everything that is necessary to win you as his bride and to restore you to deep and lasting friendship with your Father God.

Catching Fire

Yet how cold our hearts so often still are! What will ignite the wet tinder of our souls with an unquenchable love for God? Paradoxically, it happens as we see more and more our own brokenness and sin. If we view ourselves as a great acquisition and think that surely God must be blessed to have followers like us, then our love to him will indeed be small. But when the truth about our hearts becomes visible to us as the height and breadth and depth of our sin starts to be exposed, and we come to realize that God loves us still and that he died to pay even for the sins of someone like us, then our hearts start to warm. As we grow in our grasp of the magnitude of how much we have been forgiven, then our hearts begin to spark into flame, for as Jesus said, "He who is forgiven little, loves little" (Luke 7:47).

Perhaps human love can only be as strong as death, but God's love is greater still, stronger than Sheol. God's love for us in Christ has triumphed over the grave once and for all, and so in him we, too, can one day triumph over the grave, through the solid hope that he gives of the resurrection of the dead. In heaven, spouses, friends, and families will be reunited, with all their former sins and brokenness gone, replaced with a purity of love that for now we can only dream about. In Christ, we have a relationship with God and with one another that extends beyond this life into eternity and onward, a friendship on fire that we can never lose because it depends on his perfect, jealous love that will never let us go. Our love comes and goes, but his love never fails. Our names are inscribed in the wounds on the palms of his hands; they are impressed on his heart like a seal so that he can no more forget us than a mother can forget her nursing child (Isa. 49:15).

The Bible calls us all to respond to such incredible love and become friends on fire toward one another. If we are married, such self-sacrificing and passionate love is to mark out our relationship in an exclusive and powerful way. Whether married or single, we are all to love the God who calls us his bride with that kind of friendship on fire, seeking first his kingdom and laying down our lives daily for one another in obedience to his commands. Sometimes we may succeed in being such a friend; often, we will fail. In those many moments of failure, we will need to return constantly to the perfect obedience of Christ in our place, and to the cross, the place where God demonstrated his friendship on fire for us. There Jesus paid for our many failures to be the spouse that we were meant to be, and for our spouse's failures to love us as he or she ought. There Jesus paid for the coldness and indifference that we so often show to our heavenly Spouse, to Jesus himself. There at the cross and especially in the resurrection, God's fiery love triumphed forever over the grave and won the victory for his people.

In that truth—the truth of God's victory in Christ over sin and death and hell—we can find the faith to step out once again in trying to show friendship on fire to one another after we have failed many times, as well as faith in God's unbreakable love for us in Christ. There at the cross we find hope: the hope of an eternal future together with Christ from which even the flooding waters of death cannot separate us. There at the cross we find something even greater than faith and hope. We find the greatest of these, love—God's amazing, fiery love to us in the gospel.

12

The Song That Never Ends

Song of Songs 8:7–14

Woman
7 Many waters are not able to extinguish love,
and rivers cannot drown it.
Even if a man should give all the wealth of his house as the price of love,
he would be utterly scorned.

Brothers
8 We have a little sister,
and she does not [yet] have breasts.
What shall we do for our sister
on the day when she will be spoken for?
9 If she is a wall,
we would build upon her a battlement of silver;
if she is a door,
we will enclose her with a panel of cedar.

Woman
10 I was a wall,
and my breasts were like towers.
Now I have become in his eyes
one who brings peace.

11 Solomon owned a vineyard in Baal-hamon.
He gave the vineyard to keepers;
each would bring as the price of its fruit one thousand [shekels of] silver.
12 My vineyard belongs to me; it is my very own.
You may keep the thousand [shekels], O Solomon,
along with two hundred [that go] for the keepers of its fruit.

Man
13 You who dwell in gardens,
companions are listening attentively for your voice.
Cause me to hear [it]!

Woman
14 Flee, my beloved,
and be like a gazelle
or a young stag upon the mountains of perfumes.

When our children were small, one of their favorite songs was "The Song That Never Ends." Perhaps you know it. It has that title because the last line of the song merges right back into the beginning, so that once you have started to sing it, there is literally no way to gracefully bring it to a conclusion. Wherever you stop, you are always halting in midflow, so it is, quite literally, the song that never ends.

In contrast, most novelists try to bring their story to a satisfying conclusion. They tie up all the loose ends in the plot and then conclude by saying, "Reader, I married him," "And so they lived happily ever after," or the like. Perhaps surprisingly, the ending of the Song of Songs belongs much more in the first category than the second. It does not close with a neat and tidy conclusion but rather with a return to the beginning, picking up some of the central themes from along the journey and rounding off in a way that leaves us hungry for more. That is not accidental, nor is it the product of poor literary technique. Rather, it is a deliberate strategy to push us to think about the nature of the life of love that the poet has described throughout this book, in terms of both our human relationships and our relationship with God.

The Brothers

In Song 8:8, we are reintroduced to the woman's brothers, whom we met in the opening chapter but who have dropped out of sight since then. The poems in the Song do not follow a strict chronological sequence but flash back and forward as they illustrate different themes or aspects of love. The woman's brothers were a negative influence earlier in the book, and not much has changed. In the opening poem, they compelled the woman to work in the vineyards, where she was scorched by the hot sun, darkening her complexion in a way that was reckoned unattractive in that culture (1:6). In this poem, the strategy is the opposite, but the goal is the same: to maximize the woman's value for them, as if she were an object. Notice that they do not speak *to* the woman but *about* her, as if she were not present and her opinions did not matter. After all, they still regard her as "little," which in the Mishnah is a legal term describing a child under twelve years old.

In the brothers' eyes, the girl had not yet reached puberty, which would be marked by the appearance of her breasts. But they were already thinking about the day when she would be "spoken for"—when some man would come along to claim her for himself by offering a suitable bride price in exchange (Song 8:8). There are two possible interpretations of what the brothers say next, depending on what they mean by the metaphors of a "wall" and a "door." One possibility is that these are contrasting images of sexual purity: a wall represents closedness and therefore sexual purity, while an open door represents promiscuity. Thus, if she is pure, they will build up and adorn her wall with additional battlements of silver. But if she is inclined to be an open door, unchaste, they will protect her with boards of cedar.[1]

This reading puts a positive angle on the brothers' concern for the woman: certainly families ought to have such care for and interest in the sexual well-being of their younger members. Yet it is doubtful that this is the focus of what they are saying here. Doors can be shut as well as open, and the primary function of both the battlements of silver and the boards of cedar is adornment rather than enhancing the strength of the defenses. Rather, the brothers' thought seems to be that even though right now the woman might be as flat-chested as a wall or a door, with a little suitable decoration (battlements of silver or adornments of cedar), she could perhaps still be turned into a marketable commodity. Do not miss the connection with the previous verse, which speaks derisively about the purchase of love (Song 8:7), and the negative role that silver plays in the following poem about Solomon's

1. So, for example, Roland E. Murphy, *The Song of Songs: A Commentary on the Canticles or Song of Songs*, Hermeneia (Minneapolis: Fortress, 1990), 198.

vineyard (v. 11). The brothers are treating the woman in exactly the same way that the suitor of verse 7 would: as an object to be made presentable for sale to the highest bidder, no matter what her thoughts and feelings on the subject are. On that day, she will be "spoken for" (v. 8), rather than having any voice of her own.

The woman scorns their efforts. The brothers are as blind as they are deceived. She declares that she is a wall with breasts like towers (Song 8:10). In other words, she picks up both potential meanings of the metaphor and transforms them to make an entirely different point. She is not flat-chested and immature like an ordinary wall. Rather, her "wall" already has prominent towers. She doesn't need the brothers' adornment to make her attractive. God has given her all the assets that she needs. Yet at the same time, the military and defensive nature of these metaphors highlights the fact that she has not been promiscuous with her natural advantages. She has not stirred up love before it pleased. She has carefully protected her virginity until the time was right.

What is more, that right time has nothing to do with her brothers and their schemes to find a suitor for her (and benefit themselves financially). She finds her beloved without their assistance and surrenders to him, becoming for him the one who brings or finds (the word could mean either,[2] and the ambiguity may be deliberate) peace and wholeness (Song 8:10). She has become bone of his bone and flesh of his flesh, completing him and being completed by him in a way that is totally incompatible with the brothers' commercial view of marriage. She becomes a true lifetime soulmate for the man that *she* has chosen, not merely a beautiful and expensive trophy to be acquired by the highest bidder.

The Song of the Vineyards

The same themes of love and money run through in the second vignette, a song about two vineyards—Solomon's vineyard and hers. Solomon, we are told, owned a vineyard in Baal-hamon (Song 8:11). No such place is mentioned elsewhere in the Bible, so the significance of the place is likely contained in the meaning of the name, which could literally be translated "husband of a crowd." Not coincidentally, the same Hebrew word for

2. Depending on whether it is a qal form of *yatsa'* or a hiphil form of *matsa'*.

"crowd" is used in 2 Chronicles 11:23 to describe the multitude of women that Solomon's son Rehoboam acquired as wives for his sons. Likewise, Solomon's "vineyard" here represents his harem. He does not have a personal relationship of tending and caring for his vineyard but instead employs "keepers," who bring him a thousand shekels of silver for it, probably a reference to his famous seven hundred wives and three hundred concubines (1 Kings 11:3; cf. Song 6:8–9). Solomon's "vineyard" is a status symbol of his enormous wealth, power, and sexual promiscuity.

In contrast to the unbelievably valuable vineyard of Solomon, the woman, too, has a vineyard of her own (Song 8:12). Hers may not be nearly comparable to Solomon's in its monetary value, but what makes it special is the fact that it is all hers. She would rather have her own simple vineyard and the freedom to give it to the man that she chooses—a man with whom she has a real relationship—than to have Solomon's expensive vineyard, which has to be managed for him by tenants for a fee. True love cannot be bought and sold as a commercial or political transaction, not even by the most famous and wealthy of Israel's kings. Wives cannot be managed like battery-farmed chickens. True love is indeed more valuable than all the silver of Solomon's house.

Flee to the Mountains

The third vignette is perhaps the most enigmatic of all. Fittingly, the poem closes with a return to a dialogue between the man and the woman. But what does he mean when he says, "You who dwell in gardens, companions are listening attentively for your voice. Cause me to hear [it]!" (Song 8:13)? And what does she mean when she replies, "Flee, my beloved, and be like a gazelle or a young stag upon the mountains of perfumes" (v. 14)? To begin with, the woman is called a *garden-dweller*, a beautiful flower whose natural habitat is the carefully manicured environment of a king's royal estate. Remember that in antiquity, gardens were not something that everyone had in front of their homes. They were the exotic preserve of the rich. Yet this woman doesn't need to be part of the harem of a king to be a garden-dweller. Her beauty naturally gives her that status in her man's eyes. The garden is the sphere of love in the Song, so to dwell there permanently is to be constantly surrounded by love.

The reference in Song 8:13 to the companions who are listening attentively for her voice recalls 1:7, where the same term described the man's fellow shepherds. Here they represent the wider society, eagerly desiring to hear her voice, so that they, too, may understand the lessons of love that she has learned. Their listening posture invites us to listen and learn as well. The man also longs to hear the woman's voice, so he echoes his own earlier request from 2:14: "Let me hear your voice." Even after they have been married for some time, he still longs to experience her unique presence and undivided attention, just as he did before they were united together. He is as captivated by her charms as ever.

And the woman still desires him. So why does she tell him to "flee"[3] (Song 8:14) after he has asked to be with her and hear her voice? Just as the man quoted himself from chapter 2, so she quotes her own words from the same chapter in reply. Paradoxically, the place to which she sends him away is her own body, represented by the "mountains of spices" (8:14 ESV). She knows that the separations of life can never really take them away from each other. He has to leave sometimes, but only in order to return in due course and enjoy the pleasures of a gazelle on the mountains of spices, a vivid image of the delights of lovemaking (v. 14; see 2:17). A love that cannot ever let the beloved out of a person's sight is immature and insecure. The tension between longed-for togetherness and necessary separations runs throughout this chapter, just as it does in every healthy relationship. True love is able to send the beloved away, in order to receive him back in due course. Absence only makes the heart grow fonder. In this movement of leaving and returning, there is an acknowledgment that love is not a still-life painting but a dynamic, ongoing relationship, truly a song that never ends.

In other words, far from marriage extinguishing the spark of romance between the man and the woman, it has simply lit the fuse for an ongoing passion that continues to burn. The end of the Song is not the end of their godly love affair. It is merely the end of one chapter in an enduring relationship. Just as the Song began by shattering gender stereotypes, with the woman's passionate desire for the man to kiss her with the kisses of his mouth (Song 1:2), so, too, it ends with a similar shattering of stereotypes. The man desires conversation—he wants to hear the sound of her voice. The

3. Many English versions translate this as "Make haste" (ESV) or "Come away" (NIV), even though such a meaning for *bāraḥ* is not attested elsewhere in the Old Testament; see Gianni Barbiero, *Song of Songs: A Close Reading*, trans. Michael Tait, SVT 144 (Leiden: Brill, 2011), 498–501.

woman wants sex—she wants him to act like a young stag on the mountains of spices, which represent her body. Marriage is not meant to be about one (conversation) *or* the other (sex), but both together, equally prized by husband and wife alike: friendship on fire in a song that never ends.

Love and the Wider Community

These final poems remind us once again that love cannot be bought or sold; it has to be a free choice on the part of the lover and the beloved. There is a necessary tension between individuals and their social context throughout the Song. On the one hand, love cannot be coerced or purchased, whether by brothers or by potential husbands. Men do not own women. On the other hand, true love naturally longs for appropriate recognition from one's family, as demonstrated in the woman's desire earlier in the chapter to bring her man to the house of her mother. Often the challenge is balancing these two competing pressures in our lives: the desire for social approval of our relationships and the fact that love cannot be forced.

The application of this principle may be rather different in our culture than it was in an ancient culture. In their context, the issue was essentially the purchasing and selling of women by their husbands and families. A woman would be "spoken for" by her father or her brothers, who had a commercial interest in the marital transaction. She herself often had little power or say in the process. That is not typically how marriage happens in our culture. We are generally free to choose to date and marry whomever we wish. Though there are still families that exert toxic pressures on their children in this regard, we are more often likely to err by failing to heed the sound counsel of those around us, rushing into ill-advised relationships that make perfect sense to us, but that friends and family recognize to be unwise.

Though family pressures toward arranged marriages have diminished, we should not imagine for a moment that the commercialization of sex has disappeared in our culture. There are still plenty of people who want to speak for you by pressuring you into a sexual relationship that is unhealthy and undesirable. Now, instead of financially motivated brothers, who at least had a vested interest in protecting their sister's purity, we live in a context in which society pressures people into sexually charged relationships from elementary school onward. In our culture, the appearance of a girl's breasts (and the corresponding changes as boys become men) no longer functions as a sign for the family to plan a marriage, but rather as a sign that she is supposedly ready to engage in sexual activity whenever and wherever her hormones dictate. Whereas their culture separated marriage from passion, we have separated passion from marriage. In the process, both contexts lose sight of what sex is for. It is a precious gift of God that exists in service of a unique, lifelong, committed bond between one man and one woman in which she both brings and finds peace in his eyes. Sex is designed to bond a couple together in marriage so that she completes him and he completes her. As the book of Genesis puts it, "Therefore a man shall leave his father and his mother and hold fast to his wife, and they shall become one flesh" (Gen. 2:24).

Sex and the Church

These themes of sex, marriage, and society raise some powerful challenges to how we approach these topics within the church. Much of the time, we act just like the alternative interpretation of the woman's brothers. We are deeply concerned that our young women might be doors and not walls—sexually promiscuous rather than sexually restrained. Often we seem to view protecting their purity simply as an external matter of heightening the battlements and boarding up the gates. Perhaps this is because we are not so much concerned for the hearts of our sisters and daughters as we are for their marriageability. We therefore make detailed rules about all the things that nice Christian young women are not supposed to do, without ever addressing what all those intense feelings and emotions in their hearts are actually for. As parents, we can heavily invest our pride in the purity of our children, so we act as though sexual sin were the one truly unforgivable sin, a sin that ruins someone for life.

The result of such a law-heavy approach to the subject is that we easily become sexual legalists, whether of the successful or unsuccessful variety. Successful sexual legalists proudly keep all the rules, though we are often skilled at finding the technical loopholes—all the activities that don't count as sex because the "door" wasn't actually entered. What is more, our motives often have little to do with desiring to please God and much more with feeding the idol of satisfying our parents' hopes or of finding our value in our personal self-control. Meanwhile, those of us who are unsuccessful legalists feel crushed by our failures. We know that we have been doors, not walls, whether we have failed once or repeatedly, and we feel deeply the concomitant message from our families and our churches that we are now damaged goods. Who will ever "speak for us" and be interested in a relationship, now that we have had to return our silver purity ring?

Meanwhile, the commercialization of sex continues apace. In our culture, one doesn't have to be a Solomon to have a harem of a thousand women. An innumerable host of women are waiting for you at the other end of your Internet connection. These days, women too often get drawn into the pornography trap. But like Solomon with his harem, what you get out of that abundance of available pseudo-sex is not richness but emptiness. When you view pornography, you sell your soul for a bowl full of ashes, buying guilt and bondage in place of the beauty and excitement that you imagined it would deliver. We end up emptier than ever, starving for the satisfying relationship and real intimacy that we were made to enjoy and for which we deeply long.

Purity and Marriage

This passage teaches us that virginity is valuable not as an end in itself, but as a means to prepare for the surrender and peace that can be found only in the unique bond of marriage. God's law of purity before marriage is intended for our flourishing, not our frustration. Virginity before marriage is healthy, not just as a way of avoiding various diseases but as a means of protecting the bonding mechanism of the heart so that when we do marry, we are ready to find and to give peace and wholeness to our spouses.

The young woman in the Song has all the feelings and hormones that go with this stage of life. She knows what it is to want to kiss and be kissed back, to hunger for a rendezvous on the mountains of spices. But she also knows what it is to resist those desires. When she says, "I was a wall and my breasts were like towers" (Song 8:10), she is using a military metaphor. In antiquity, the towers were a key part of the city's defenses, and so protecting them was crucial to the safety of the city. Once the towers fell, the city was defenseless. So, too, this young woman has not merely remained a virgin technically; she has protected her honor carefully. Yet there is no glorification of virginity as a higher and more spiritual state. She guarded the walls and towers of her city well so that when the right time came to surrender, she could do so in a way that would bring her (and her husband) peace and wholeness, not guilt and shame. Sex is such a precious and beautiful gift within marriage that she wanted to be able to share it with her husband without the baggage that can come from past sexual relationships.

In the biblical context, the image of virginity as a defended city also addresses the temptation to sexual legalism, whether of the successful or unsuccessful variety. To successful legalists, the image of a defended city refutes our pride. After all, as Psalm 127:1 reminds us, unless the Lord defends the city, the watchman stays awake in vain. So if you are sexually pure, it is not your doing, or something in which you can boast and take pride. It is the Lord's work. There are typically many different components in a person's purity. Perhaps you grew up in a healthy family with good role models and became a Christian at an early age. What credit do you deserve for that? Perhaps you have come from a sheltered background, or perhaps you are a person with naturally strong willpower. Who gave you those things? Or maybe you are, as I was as a teenager, socially awkward and not particularly physically attractive. What a gift of God's mercy! If you are sexually pure, it is entirely the result of the Lord's kindness to you, something to give thanks for rather than to take pride in.

But if you are sexually broken, the image of purity as a defended city also gives you hope. For when God's people rebelled against him, his own chosen city of Jerusalem was given over to invaders. They tore down its walls and ransacked its towers, creating havoc within. Yet that was not the end of the story for that city. The Lord would not give his city up, in spite of her sin and devastation. He committed himself to create a New Jerusalem, whose filthy garments would be replaced by clothing of spotless purity.

In the same way, the Lord can take your broken-down, undefended city and transform it by his grace into a place where peace and purity reign. When we act as though giving in to sexual temptation ruins us for life and is a sin from which we cannot recover, we are forgetting the gospel of God's grace, and may alienate those who most need our love and support. The truth is that God can use sexual temptation and failure to bring us to a deeper understanding and appreciation of our need for his grace: our struggle with same-sex attraction, pornography, adultery, or other forms of sexual sin may be the means by which the gospel shines more brightly in our lives. God can help us to rebuild the broken-down walls of our lives and to begin to guard the towers once again. He may ultimately even enable us to find peace in a biblical marriage relationship as an undeserved gift, in spite of our past failures. There is hope for the sexually broken, just as there is for all of us who are broken in other ways.

Nonetheless, it is in the context of a unique and committed relationship of marriage that sex finds its proper and delightful place. This is the point of the concluding couplet. Many people find the woman's company attractive, but she belongs to one man, who longs for the opportunity to enjoy her conversation. Nor is their relationship simply about good conversation and deep friendship, so that they walk through life gazing together in the same direction. In the midst of the busyness of life and everyday duties, she takes the time to stop and to face him, looking deeply into his eyes. She desires to get away from it all with him and delight once again in his caresses. Her breasts, which were once strongly defended towers, have now been transformed into mountains of spices on which he may eagerly frolic like a young stag.

An Ongoing Song

Just when we expect the "and so they lived happily ever after," it doesn't come. There is no neat conclusion to the Song because love doesn't end neatly and tidily. It is an ongoing relationship, a song that never ends. That is one of several things that connect the message of this poem about human relationships with our relationship to our heavenly Bridegroom. To be sure, there are fundamental differences between the two relationships. The woman in the Song asserts her right to choose freely for herself the man whom she will love, but we have an obligation to love our heavenly Husband, who is our Creator and Sovereign Lord. It is not left up to us to choose whom we will serve. He made us, and we belong to him. Yet our Creator has not presumed to rest in the fact that we are obligated to love him because everything we are and have comes from him. God could simply have demanded that we fall down and worship him, but instead he woos us with his tender love for us. His love for humanity was demonstrated from the moment of creation, when he made this magnificent world and placed humanity at its pinnacle, as the crowning glory of his creation. God made a good and beautiful world; then he made us to be "garden-dwellers," preparing a glorious royal Paradise in Genesis for the first man and the first woman. He sought out Adam and Eve daily for fellowship with him, listening for their voice.

How have we responded to such great love? We have been spiritually adulterous from the beginning. Our first parents listened to the voice of the serpent and abandoned the way of wisdom. Ever since then, we have been doors and not walls when it comes to protecting our hearts against the advances of the evil one. Far from carefully protecting our spiritual chastity so that we could offer it as a gift to our faithful Husband, we engage daily in spiritual prostitution, following other gods that promise us peace and wholeness in the things that matter most to us. Our idols swear that they will grant us success, significance, and safety. But they lie, leaving all of us with broken-down walls and demolished towers, wondering where peace is to be found. We have sold our vineyard to the highest bidder, only to find that payment was made in counterfeit currency.

For some, spiritual adultery takes place quite literally in the sexual realm. We have pursued sex outside the bounds of marriage, with our minds and with our bodies. We have lusted, and sometimes acted out those fantasies in reality, ending up feeling ashamed and dirty. We thought that sex would bring us intimacy, value, and meaning, only to discover that we had been sold a bill of goods. For others, spiritual adultery has taken place in quite other realms. Perhaps we have pursued academic or career success, lavishing our attentions and our enthusiasm on our ambitions, while we neglect the God who made us and gave us those gifts. Or we have made people into our gods, desperately pursuing their approval and utterly distraught if they disdain us. Or we show no interest in others whatsoever, believing the line from Oscar Wilde that "to love oneself is the beginning of a lifelong romance."[4] We idolize our comfort and security, and we sacrifice anything that might threaten them. We may have pursued different means, but the idols often turn out to be exactly the same.

There are many ways in which we commit spiritual adultery, and none of us can claim to be genuinely pure in heart and body. We can even use whatever outward purity we have as a source of pride and a functional denial

4. Spoken by Lord Goring in Oscar Wilde's play *An Ideal Husband* (London: Dover Publications, 2000), 46.

of our need of the gospel. But God has nonetheless loved us in a remarkable way. We do not have a Husband who purchased for himself a faithful and pure virgin for a bride. Instead, as the story of Hosea and Gomer so dramatically illustrates, we have a Husband who so loved his broken and impure bride that he went after us in our adulterous wanderings and purchased us back. The cost to acquire us was not paid with perishable things such as silver and cedar, but rather with his own blood. The blood of Jesus, shed on the cross, cleanses away all our impurity—sexual and otherwise. His perfect and faithful love for God the Father and for his neighbor while he lived in this broken world creates the pure robe of righteousness that we need to approach a holy God. He comes to us, the undeserving bride, clothing us in beauty and listening for our voice, desiring to have a deep and genuine relationship with us. That is true friendship on fire. There is a love that indeed will not let us go. That is a song that truly never ends. Many waters cannot quench such love, nor can the rivers drown it. Death itself has no power over such love!

Responding to God's Love

So how will you respond to God's amazing love? Perhaps you have not responded to him before. You are still married to your idols, even though they treat you like a slave and constantly leave you deeply unsatisfied. Leave them, and come to the true Lover of your souls. Give your heart and life over to him, and find in him a true peace that transcends the difficulty of your present circumstances. He is the One for whom you were made, and in whom is fullness of life. Do not delay any longer. Throw yourself eagerly into his outstretched loving arms.

If you are a Christian already, ponder his great and enduring love for you, which is the ground and motivation for your love for him and for those around you. Marriage is difficult. Sinners can and do hurt each other regularly. There will be times when the last thing you desire is to hear your spouse's voice or to journey to the mountains of spices with him or her. Time and time again, you will need to come back to your heavenly Bridegroom's love for you to stir your heart afresh for your spouse.

Purity is hard as well, whether you are single or married. We are constantly surrounded by the forces of the evil one, who seeks to overcome the walls of our cities. Only the Lord can give us the grace to defend those walls successfully. So plead for his help in the struggle against sexual temptation in all its forms. Find other believers who will pray for you and encourage you in the fight. Find comfort in the fact that, though the earthly struggle against sin is lifelong and difficult, a day is coming when our Bridegroom will return. He is coming for his bride, the church. Our Bridegroom brings with him the reward for every faithful effort we expend and the release from the guilt of all our failures. Then we will be forever with the Lord, not in a garden like Eden but in a redeemed, restored, and beautified city, the garden-city of the New Jerusalem.

On that day, the bride's eyes will not be on herself but on the Beloved for whom she waits. As Anne R. Cousin so beautifully expressed it in her hymn:

> The bride eyes not her garment, but her dear bridegroom's face;
> I will not gaze at glory, but on my King of grace;
> Not at the crown he gifteth, but on his pierced hand:
> The Lamb is all the glory of Emmanuel's land.[5]

On that day, Jesus will finally say to us: "Arise, my love, my beautiful one, and come away, for behold, the winter is past; the rain is over and gone. The flowers appear on the earth, [and] the time of singing has come" (Song 2:10–12 ESV). On that day, we will finally know that "my beloved is mine, and I am his" (v. 16): we will be his and he will be ours, forever and forever.

5. "The Sands of Time Are Sinking" (1857).

Bibliography

Assis, Elie. *Flashes of Fire: A Literary Analysis of the Song of Songs*. New York: T. & T. Clark, 2009.

Augustine. *Confessions*. Translated by E. B. Pusey. New York: E. P. Dutton & Co., 1949.

Banks, Iain M. *The Crow Road*. London: Scribners, 1992.

Barbiero, Gianni. *Song of Songs: A Close Reading*. Translated by Michael Tait. SVT 144. Leiden: Brill, 2011.

Brooks, Richard. *Song of Songs*. Fearn, UK: Christian Focus, 1999.

Carr, G. Lloyd. *The Song of Solomon: An Introduction and Commentary*. TOTC 17. Downers Grove, IL: InterVarsity Press, 1984.

Clines, D. J. A. "Why Is There a Song of Songs and What Does It Do to You If You Read It?" In *Interested Parties: The Ideology of Writers and Readers of the Hebrew Bible*, edited by P. R. Davies and D. J. A. Clines, 94–121. JSOTS 205. Sheffield, UK: Sheffield Academic Press, 1995.

Davis, Ellen F. *Proverbs, Ecclesiastes, and the Song of Songs*. Westminster Bible Companion. Louisville, KY: Westminster John Knox, 2000.

———. "Romance of the Land in the Song of Songs." *ATR* 80 (1998): 533–46.

Dillow, Joseph. *Solomon on Sex*. Nashville: Thomas Nelson, 1982.

Donne, John. "Holy Sonnets, 14." In *The Complete English Poems*. London: Penguin, 1977.

Duguid, Iain M. *Is Jesus in the Old Testament?* Phillipsburg, NJ: P&R Publishing, 2013.

———. *The Song of Songs: An Introduction and Commentary*. TOTC 19. Downers Grove, IL: InterVarsity Press, 2015.

Durham, James. *The Song of Solomon*. 1668. Reprint, Edinburgh: Banner of Truth, 1982.

Exum, J. Cheryl. *Song of Songs: A Commentary*. OTL. Louisville, KY: Westminster John Knox, 2005.

Fox, Michael V. *The Song of Songs and the Ancient Egyptian Love Songs*. Madison, WI: University of Wisconsin Press, 1985.

Fredericks, Daniel C., and Daniel J. Estes. *Ecclesiastes & the Song of Songs*. AOTC 16. Downers Grove, IL: InterVarsity Press, 2010.

Freud, Sigmund. *Totem and Taboo*. London: Routledge, 1950.

Glickman, Craig. *Solomon's Song of Love: Let a Song of Songs Inspire Your Own Love Story*. Brentwood, TN: Howard, 2004.

Goldsworthy, Graeme. *Preaching the Whole Bible as Christian Scripture*. Grand Rapids: Eerdmans, 2000.

Henry, Matthew. *Matthew Henry's Commentary*. Peabody, MA: Hendrickson, 1991.

Hess, Richard S. *Song of Songs*. BCOTWP. Grand Rapids: Baker Academic, 2005.

Horine, Steven. *Interpretive Images in the Song of Songs: From Wedding Chariots to Bridal Chambers*. New York: Peter Lang, 2001.

Keel, Othmar. *The Song of Songs: A Continental Commentary*. Minneapolis: Fortress, 1994.

Lee, Bruce. *Artist of Life*. Edited by John Little. Boston: Tuttle, 1999.

Lewis, C. S. *Christian Reflections*. Grand Rapids: Eerdmans, 1994.

———. *Mere Christianity*. London: G. Bles, 1969.

Longman, Tremper, III. *Song of Songs*. NICOT. Grand Rapids: Eerdmans, 2001.

Miller, Don. *Blue like Jazz: Nonreligious Thoughts on Christian Spirituality*. Nashville: Thomas Nelson, 2003.

Miller, Shannon Hodde. "'Am I Pretty?' A Troubling Question among Christian Women like Me." *CT* (March 9, 2012). http://www.christianitytoday.com/women/2012/march/am-i-pretty-troubling-question-among-christian-women-like.html?paging=off.

Mitchell, Christopher. *The Song of Songs*. St. Louis: Concordia, 2003.

Murphy, Roland E. *The Song of Songs: A Commentary on the Canticles or Song of Songs*. Hermeneia. Minneapolis: Fortress, 1990.

O'Donnell, Douglas Sean. *Song of Solomon*. Preaching the Word. Wheaton, IL: Crossway, 2012.

Powlison, David, and John Yenchko. *Pre-Engagement: Five Questions to Ask Yourselves*. Phillipsburg, NJ: P&R Publishing, 2000.

Regnerus, Mark. “The Case for Early Marriage.” *CT* (July 31, 2009). http://www.christianitytoday.com/ct/2009/august/16.22.html.

Segrave, Kerry. *Suntanning in 20th Century America*. Jefferson, NC: McFarland & Company, 2005.

Smith, Alexander McCall. The No. 1 Ladies’ Detective Agency series. Edinburgh: Polygon, 1998–2003. Various other publishers and dates.

Van der Toorn, Karel. “The Significance of the Veil in the Ancient Near East.” In *Pomegranates and Golden Bells: Studies in Biblical, Jewish, and Near Eastern Ritual, Law, and Literature in Honor of Jacob Milgrom*, edited by David P. Wright, David Noel Freedman, and Avi Hurvitz, 327–40. Winona Lake, IN: Eisenbrauns, 1995.

Walsh, Carey Ellen. *Exquisite Desire: Religion, the Erotic, and the Song of Songs*. Minneapolis: Fortress, 2000.

Wilde, Oscar. *An Ideal Husband*. London: Dover Publications, 2000.

Index of Scripture

Index of Subjects and Names

Available in the Reformed Expository Commentary Series

Old Testament

Genesis, by Richard D. Phillips
1 Samuel, by Richard D. Phillips
2 Samuel, by Richard D. Phillips
1 Kings, by Philip Graham Ryken
2 Kings, by Philip Graham Ryken
Ezra & Nehemiah, by Derek W. H. Thomas
Esther & Ruth, by Iain M. Duguid
Psalms 42–72, by Richard D. Phillips
Psalms 73–106, by Richard D. Phillips
Ecclesiastes, by Douglas Sean O'Donnell
Song of Songs, by Iain M. Duguid
Daniel, by Iain M. Duguid
Hosea, by Richard D. Phillips
Jonah & Micah, by Richard D. Phillips
Zephaniah, Haggai, and Malachi, by Iain M. Duguid and Matthew P. Harmon
Zechariah, by Richard D. Phillips

Forthcoming

Exodus, by William B. Barcley
Deuteronomy, by Trent Casto
Psalms 1–41, by Iain M. Duguid and James Duguid